Literacy Success for Emergent Bilinguals

GETTING IT RIGHT IN THE PREK–2 CLASSROOM

THERESA A. ROBERTS

TEACHERS COLLEGE PRESS
TEACHERS COLLEGE | COLUMBIA UNIVERSITY
NEW YORK AND LONDON

Published by Teachers College Press, 1234 Amsterdam Avenue, New York, NY 10027

Copyright © 2017 by Teachers College, Columbia University

Cover design by David K. Kessler. Photos by monkeybusinessimages, Yagi-Studio, and fstop123, all via iStock by Getty Images.

All rights reserved. No part of this publication may be reproduced or transmitted in any form or by any means, electronic or mechanical, including photocopy, or any information storage and retrieval system, without permission from the publisher.

Library of Congress Cataloging-in-Publication Data

Names: Roberts, Theresa A.
Title: Literacy success for emergent bilinguals : getting it right in the preK–2 classroom / Theresa A. Roberts.
Description: New York, NY : Teachers College Press, 2017. | Series: Common core state standards in literacy series | Includes bibliographical references and index.
Identifiers: LCCN 2016045004 (print) | LCCN 2016046295 (ebook) | ISBN 9780807758175 (pbk.) | ISBN 9780807775585 (ebook)
Subjects: LCSH: English language—Study and teaching (Early childhood)—Foreign speakers.
Classification: LCC PE1128.A2 R543 2017 (print) | LCC PE1128.A2 (ebook) | DDC 372.65/1—dc23
LC record available at https://lccn.loc.gov/2016045004

ISBN 978-0-8077-5817-5 (paper)
ISBN 978-0-8077-7558-5 (ebook)

Printed on acid-free paper

Manufactured in the United States of America

24 23 22 21 20 19 18 17 8 7 6 5 4 3 2 1

Contents

Preface

Students who come to us with primary languages other than English challenge us to appreciate and leverage the assets that they bring in order to help them emerge as successful bilingual and multilingual learners. It is the purpose of this book to help teachers do just that. Although these students have long been referred to as English language learners or ELLs, terminology is changing as we recognize that these students learn best when they are encouraged to maintain and use their original languages while acquiring English. The educator's goal is not to replace students' first language but rather to help them add a second language and, in so doing, create a combined language reservoir that yields academic, social, and economic strengths. To this end, we use the term *emergent bilingual* (EB) in the book, as well as the acronyms EBs (emergent bilinguals), EBS (emergent bilingual students), and EBL (emergent bilingual learners).

I hope this book will encourage and help you to take a fresh and serious look at English language arts PreK–2 programs and instructional practices in your school. I want to help you envision and enact instructional modifications that can maximally support the achievement of EBLs. It is certainly the case that the English language arts competencies of EBLs can be promoted by the practices that occur within your classroom. It is also true that effective educational programs for EBLs require educators to proactively shape their school and district organization into ones with a hopeful, educationally effective, and positive sustained stance toward EBLs and their families and communities. As has been elegantly and simply stated, "It takes a village."

Each chapter contains ideas that have substantial amounts of supporting research or high promise, relevance to classroom practice, and potential for increasing EBLs' achievement in English language and literacy. For all the chapter topics I explain the *why*, supplemented with illustrations of the *how*. The chapter content can be briefly described as follows:

1. The first chapter describes the broad and interacting educational, cultural, social, and economic factors that influence school achievement. I point out the importance of accounting for these influences and suggest educational policies and practices to do so. The importance of alliances with families to bridge school and home with respect to these factors is described.

2. Children's deep connection to their first language and the multiple ways its utilization in schools can contribute to language and literacy achievement is detailed in this chapter. I discuss effective and realistic practices for increasing the use of first language in classrooms where children speak multiple languages and teachers speak few of them.
3. In this chapter, the manner in which children acquire a first language, based on the most recent research, is explained as a simple three-part process. I present the central role played by teacher-student interaction and methods of classroom organization to strengthen English proficiency.
4. The important dimensions of language structure that emergent bilinguals need for language and literacy success are explained in this chapter, with many examples to illustrate effective classroom practices for teaching language structure. I highlight the contributions to learning language structure that can be made through children's language production related to meaningful ideas and topics, correction, and peer collaboration.
5. In this chapter, I explain the reasons why strong reading foundations are critically important for emergent bilinguals and are deserving of significant instructional time in PreK–2. I identify common instructional methods to be used for teaching alphabetics, phonemic awareness, and word reading, which are all particularly supportive for emergent bilinguals' reading success.
6. This chapter provides teaching guidance on the questions of *what* vocabulary to teach and *how* to increase vocabulary learning through instruction and during more informal vocabulary learning opportunities. I emphasize the importance of a cohesive, explicit, and organized vocabulary scope and sequence in PreK–2 for ensuring that emergent bilinguals have sufficient English vocabulary for language and literacy success.
7. Core strategies for comprehending and thinking that are effective and accessible for emergent bilingual children are presented in this chapter. Specific attention is devoted to the topics of how to teach close reading, how to use the first language to support comprehension and thinking, and how to balance the use of narrative and informational text.
8. The goal of this chapter is to help teachers increase the use of classroom practices that support emergent bilinguals' emotionally positive and self-sustaining motivation for language and literacy learning. I explain the research on how teacher praise and achievement-related statements, evaluation practices, and the organization of student learning and collaboration can increase motivation for language and literacy, and suggest many immediately applicable practices.

At the beginning of each chapter, I present *Important Research Findings* pertaining to the chapter topic. Throughout the chapters, general school, district, and program *educational principles* and especially classroom *teaching practices* are offered. Having these practices in your toolbox will help you generate specific activities embodying that practice that fit the multifaceted nature of the EBs you teach. At the end of each chapter, the principles and practices are summarized, inviting many quick reviews. Individual *Apply Your Knowledge* exercises are included throughout each chapter. The purpose of these exercises is to help you evaluate, sharpen, and deepen your understanding and instructional competence with the key ideas presented in the text. Each chapter also includes a list of ideas for how to engage families as true partners in supporting student learning related to the specific topic of that chapter.

The scope of the book is bold in my ambition to establish continuity across the 4- to 5-year span from PreK–Grade 2. This continuity is needed for establishing a strong foundation for EBLs' language and literacy achievement. I hope that each of you, whether you are a PreK educator or K–2 educator, will attend equally to the PreK and K–2 portions of each chapter, as this could powerfully contribute to turning vision to reality for PreK–2 language and literacy continuity in the schools where you teach. Each chapter closes with discussions of the PreK–Grade 2 Continuum and connections to the Common Core State Standards (CCSS) and PreK standards for that chapter's topic. These connections are intended to help schools and districts in the large majority of states that have aligned their curriculum and instruction to the CCSS, even if they are not using Partnership for Assessment of Readiness for College and Careers (PARRCC) or Smarter Balance assessments. Explanation of these connections will also be helpful to schools and districts within states that have chosen to write their own standards, as there is much overlap between high-quality state standards and CCSS.

CHAPTER 1

The Multifaceted Context of Emergent Bilinguals' Achievement

Important Research Findings About the Multifaceted Context of Emergent Bilingual Achievement

- » Emergent bilinguals have linguistic, emotional, familial, and cultural Wellsprings of Promise.
- » English language proficiency is a centerpiece of EBs' academic success.
- » Psychological, cultural, sociopolitical, linguistic, and educational factors shape the academic achievement of EBs.
- » EBs are a very diverse group with respect to culture, first languages, economic circumstances, family education and literacy levels, and patterns of second language acquisition.
- » Cognitive stimulation and resources in the home are greater challenges of poverty than is social-emotional support in the home.
- » By grade 4, 69% of EBs do not read English at a basic level.
- » Two-thirds of EBs come from families with incomes below 200% of the poverty level.
- » Most teachers are Caucasian, speak only one language, and have limited professional development in teaching English language learners.
- » The PreK and K–2 systems have different funding sources, goals, and teacher workforces, and often function with little coordination.
- » Effective English language development programs have been lacking.

The achievement of emergent bilingual students is influenced by many factors. My goal in this book is to advance teacher understanding of this multifaceted context of EBs' achievement and provide concrete educational principles and practices to capitalize upon the Wellsprings of Promise within children and their families that can support language and literacy. These wellsprings include linguistic, cultural and individual resources.

Linguistic, familial, cultural, economic, and sociopolitical factors are among the most important of the broad, deep, and diverse influences that shape emergent bilinguals' development and school achievement. Some of these formative influences provide EBs with strengths they need to support language and literacy learning and should therefore be capitalized upon within classrooms. Others present challenges and obstacles to achievement. Understanding these challenges can help educators accurately identify sources of responsibility for the difficulties in language and literacy achievement that many EBs experience. Understanding can also guide educators in finding solutions to challenges and obstacles by modifying educational programs and practices. The first part of this chapter will explore the most important facets that educators need to be keenly aware of:

- Linguistic, familial, cultural and individual Wellsprings of Promise
- Current societal context and patterns of academic achievement of EBs
- Socioeconomic circumstances of children, their families, and their communities
- Variation in the patterns in which the home or first language (L1) and English (L2) are being learned
- Characteristics of educators
- Separation of PreK and K–2 educational systems
- The value of alliances with families of EBs

Awareness and understanding of this multifaceted context is a starting point on the long journey to change the historical context of EBs being at risk for school achievement into a current and future context of being at promise for school language and literacy achievement. Educators' disposition and skill to carefully, thoughtfully, consistently, and robustly respond to accommodate and draw upon these deeply rooted and influential facets as resources is foundational for EB achievement. This book focuses on supporting EBs in PreK–2 to achieve educational excellence that results in high levels of speaking, listening, reading, and writing competence. Advocacy for EBs and their families is a final part of every educator's role because of these students' underrepresented voices and the economic challenges and continuing discrimination and bias that can affect EBs and their families outside of school and, sadly, far too often within schools. The importance of creating alliances with families to enable and enrich the connection between home life and school life is elaborated upon.

In the second part of this chapter, I provide an overview of how this multifaceted portrait interfaces with the Common Core State Standards (CCSS) for English language arts (ELA) and preschool learning standards, guidelines, or frameworks. The major opportunities, challenges, and omissions of the CCSS and PreK standards and frameworks will be identified. We turn now to the happy experience of highlighting children's linguistic, familial, and cultural Wellsprings of Promise.

LINGUISTIC, FAMILIAL, AND CULTURAL WELLSPRINGS OF PROMISE

Educational Principle 1: Consistently increase the extent to which school and classroom practices draw upon children's and their families' linguistic, familial, and cultural Wellsprings of Promise.

Young emergent bilinguals enter school with several strengths deeply embedded within their core. I refer to these strengths as *Wellsprings of Promise.* When children's Wellsprings of Promise flow continuously and deeply into language and literacy learning, achievement is supported. Language and literacy programs that brilliantly incorporate all of these Wellsprings of Promise will be those where the language and literacy achievement of EBs shines. It is like a precious gem: The more facets that are cut and the better the craft in shining each facet, the greater the final brilliance.

Linguistic Development

The first Wellspring of Promise is the language children have learned in their homes and communities. Use of the language children know best at home and school allows them to function at their cognitive maturity. When children can use their first language (L1) to discuss their reactions to story characters and plots, critique the reasons an historical event occurred, or generate hypotheses for how water turns to ice, they are enabled to think more fully and at a conceptual level closer to their maximal capacity. Competence in and motivation to use their first language is necessary if children are to maximally benefit from the cultural, social, familial, and other learning opportunities available in their homes and communities (Moll, Amanti, Neff, & Gonzalez, 1992). Use of the first language for high-level thinking and other purposes in schools also adds to children's first language competence. Opportunities to use the first language in school signals to children and their families that the home language is valuable and respected. Usage will also encourage children to value this linguistic wellspring of promise and maintain their motivation to use it.

Family Support

A second wellspring of promise is children's families. All children are most often raised in families where they are loved and cared for. These positive and nurturing experiences imbue children with emotional security that encourages them to confidently move out from the family and eagerly take part in the enriching experiences they encounter, if they find similar levels of emotional support in these new contexts. In these supportive contexts, the familial Wellspring of Promise can flow and gently carry the child forward into new territory.

Research has confirmed the presence of familial resources that will support EB children's language and literacy achievement in out-of-home settings. Parents and teachers of kindergarten children estimated that the majority of both EB and English fluent (EF) children demonstrate positive social skills. Another study suggested that at-risk EB children may have social–emotional strengths greater than those of EF children (Crosnoe, 2004). The extensive social contacts and greater percentage of intact families characteristic of many groups of EBs have been suggested as possible supports for resilience and coping, even in the presence of other family stressors (Espinosa, 2006).

Cultural Context

The cultural context in which children and their families may be embedded is a third Wellspring of Promise. For some EBs, this cultural context may be similar to that of English-fluent children from families of similar economic circumstances. Many others will have extensive socialization experiences within their families and community that differ significantly from those of typical mainstream U.S. culture. This diversity may range from something as simple as what is eaten for breakfast to issues as serious and deep as medical practices and the nature of religious beliefs. Head Start has published a document titled *Multicultural Principles for Head Start Programs Serving Children Ages Birth to Five* (U.S. Department of Health and Human Services, U.S. Administration for Children and Families, 2010) that clearly elaborates educational principles related to cultural context. This document asserts that children's cultural context should be the basis for educational programming. Children's cultural context is seen as a foundational component of their background knowledge that can and should be brought to bear in what is learned, as well as in learning materials and instructional practices. In addition, PreK frameworks and standards strongly endorse the inclusion of children's home experiences. However, there are few clearly conceptualized, broad, and comprehensive program models based upon children's home experiences . There is opportunity within CCSS to include books, topics, and community materials and human resources that flow from children's Wellsprings of Promise because the CCSS do not dictate what must be taught or which practices should be used to achieve the standards. Unfortunately, there is a long history of schools failing to honor and draw upon these sources of strength (Goldenberg, 2008), although noticeable winds of change are beginning to stir. Your efforts to enact Educational Principle 1 (listed earlier) can add to that breeze.

> ***Apply Your Knowledge:*** Reflect upon the ways in which your curriculum in language and literacy, math, social studies, science, and the arts capitalizes upon children's Wellsprings of Promise. List these practices. Then identify one to two ways in which you could add to these practices in your classrooms. Begin the implementation process.

CHALLENGES TO THE ACADEMIC ACHIEVEMENT OF EMERGENT BILINGUALS

Educational Principle 2: Hold steadfast every day to high expectations and optimism for language and literacy achievement for all emergent bilinguals.

There has been a dramatic increase in the number of PreK–2 children who are acquiring and learning with both a home language and English (National Clearinghouse for English Language Acquisition, 2012). Head Start serves more than 300,000 EBs who are present in 87.4% of its classrooms (U.S. Department of Health and Human Services, Administration for Children and Families, 2012). The 2015 National Assessment of Educational Progress (NAEP) showed that fully 68% of 4th-grade EBs cannot read English at even a basic level, compared to 20% of non-EB students (National Center for Education Statistics, 2015). Other emerging evidence suggests that preschool EBs may need development in both their first language and English. These facts set off a loud alarm that should engage all educators in deep reflection and help establish an openness toward fresh and perhaps very different instructional practices for teaching language and literacy. The long history of achievement challenges, disappointment, and concern for children, families and educators has led to challenging conditions for maintaining the high expectations and optimism for a better achievement future necessary to turn possibility into reality.

Socioeconomic Circumstances

Educational Principle 3: Develop comprehensive plans and ongoing focus to help families increase the amount of cognitive stimulation in children's homes.

EB children are disproportionately overrepresented among America's poor, with the majority (66%) coming from households with incomes below 200% of the federal poverty level (Editorial Progress in Education (EPE) Research Center, 2009). Low income is a significant risk factor for school achievement. As pointed out above, most children in poor families are loved and cared for and have nurturing relationships. The greater challenge within these families is the availability of resources for cognitive stimulation (Bradley & Cervyn, 2002; McLoyd, 1998). From my experience, home visits to low-income families may reveal that a blank sheet of paper and a pen cannot be located, there are few children's books or adult literacy materials, educational games and toys in working condition are limited, and all of the surfaces in the home are taken up by things needed for daily life, leaving few spaces available for engaging in child projects or homework. In one low-income community, many preschool children who lived less than 5 miles from the local children's discovery park had never been there. The pressures and demands of providing basic necessities limits families' time and focus to engage in interactions that provide cognitive stimulation.

Research has shown that classrooms serving children and families with limited economic resources exhibit similar lacks in cognitive stimulation. The CLASS

Figure 1.1. Averages of Interactions in PreK-3 Classrooms

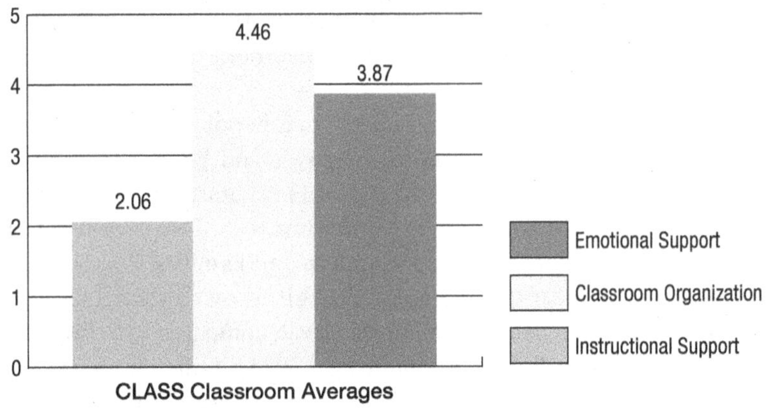

(Classroom Assessment Scoring System) is widely used in preschool classrooms and has been used somewhat in K–3 classrooms. Rigorous observational measures of emotional support, classroom organization, and instructional support are gathered using the CLASS. The level of social–emotional support found in many classrooms is high, though the level of instructional support for language and concepts is low (Mashburn, Pianta, Hamre, Downer, Barbarin, Bryant, et al., 2008) (see Figure 1.1). It appears that in both homes and classrooms an increased focus on cognitive stimulation and learning is needed.

Variation in Home and School Patterns of L1 and L2 Acquisition

Educational Principle 4: Establish programmatic policy and practices to obtain information on the patterns of L1 and L2 language use in the home.

Many preschool children will be acquiring their first language and English at the same time. Sophia and Marcos are children in a family that has just immigrated to the United States. Three-year-old Sophia is learning to speak Spanish at home, but attends a preschool where English is dominant. Sophia is learning two languages *simultaneously*. Her 8-year-old brother, Marcos, is in 2nd grade. He is accustomed to speaking Spanish at home, but has had very limited previous exposure to English. He is learning two languages *sequentially*.

Among EBs, there is substantial variability in how much L1 and L2 is used in the home. For example, approximately 50% of Head Start EBs used mostly Spanish at home, one-third used Spanish and English at home, and the remaining 17% used mostly English at home (Hindman & Wasik, 2015). There is every reason to think that this variability would also be present in K–2 families. These home differences are associated with the degree of language support children may need because greater home exposure to English is associated with faster growth in English proficiency.

Figure 1.2. Ranking of Potential Academic Success for EBs

English immersion		High-quality bilingual
Mainstream with embedded ELD	Mainstream with blocked ELD	Dual immersion
LEAST EFFECTIVE	————————>	MOST EFFECTIVE

The types of school and instructional programs within which EBs may be educated are another important contextual factor. There may be between two and 15 home languages represented within a given classroom. The languages will vary in their similarity to English, the availability of written materials in the languages, and the people who speak, read, and write them. An EB could be in a newcomer class, an English immersion class, a mainstream class with English language development (ELD), a bilingual class or a dual-immersion class. Available research allows some measure of ranking of the potential academic success for EBs depending upon which type of classrooms they attend (Kim, Hutchison & Winsler, 2013). This ranking in shown in Figure 1.2.

Characteristics of Educators

Educational Principle 5: Seek out and support the hiring of teachers who come from a wide range of cultures and language backgrounds.

Educational Principle 6: Provide teachers with the knowledge of the English language needed to effectively teach language and literacy and the support needed to develop instructional practices that are most effective for EBs.

The majority of elementary teachers are female (76%). Eighty-two percent of them are White, and a meager 8% and 2% are Hispanic or Asian, respectively. In addition, the majority of teachers of EBs have limited preparation for teaching such students (Lucas, 2011). Several studies have shown that teachers are limited in the linguistic knowledge needed to teach English language development and early reading (Cunningham, Etter, Platas, Wheeler, & Campbell, 2015; Moats, 2015). Teachers report that they are less confident of their ability to effectively teach EBs compared to EF children (Karabenick & Noda, 2004). There is both positive and worrisome evidence regarding teachers' views of EBs and the broader diversity associated with them. Some studies indicate that teachers truly appreciate the enriching potential of the diversity of EBs and are optimistic about these students' achievement potential. Other studies reveal that teachers in regular classrooms may be less supportive of using home languages in the classroom than teachers in bilingual programs. These personal, professional, knowledge and skill, and attitudinal characteristics suggest that the teaching force is not representative of the EB population in the United States, is largely underprepared to and experiencing difficulty in how to effectively teach EBs, and may have attitudes and dispositions that are unlikely to support EBs' achievement promise.

Separation of PreK and K–2 Educational Systems

Educational Principle 7: Establish the development of PreK–2 language and literacy learning continuums as a priority for the language and literacy achievement of EBs.

PreK and K–2 programs are separated by many significant factors, including the purposes of the programs, structural differences in funding, and even physical location. These programs differ with respect to the qualifications and training of educators teaching in them, the training of administrators, the learners they serve, the breadth of the developmental outcomes they aspire to, and the instructional practices they use and value. It is obvious that there are many obstacles to establishing PreK–2 continuity, although there are many benefits for language and literacy learning that could be achieved, especially for EBs. Perhaps the most important benefit would be strengthening English language development (ELD). Program continuity from PreK–2 establishes a 4- to 5-year period (the same as the lower estimate for how long it takes to acquire a moderate level of English) to plan for English development. It is an exciting dream to envision an ELD program that contains a comprehensive, thoughtful, and truly research-based scope and sequence of language development that would greet 3-year-old EBs upon preschool entry and accompany and serve them all the way through 2nd grade. Such a plan would surely establish a sequence for teaching and learning vocabulary, language structure, and meaningful language usage from PreK–Grade 2. The plan would include strands for both basic communication and academic language. It would include a scope and sequence for teaching and learning alphabet knowledge, phonological awareness, word reading, and thinking and comprehension. The plan would include ambitious monitoring of English proficiency in both the home language and English, with those results shared across years, updated regularly, and used to monitor progress to determine the types of language support needed.

There are other benefits EBs would acquire through establishing a comprehensive PreK–2 language and literacy program. These benefits include the educational enrichment that would accrue to EBs from cross-pollination between PreK and K–2 programs. PreK and K–2 have strengths that could benefit each other. PreK has a strong tradition of emphasizing social–emotional development alongside cognitive development. PreK programs strongly value family engagement, inclusion of role models from the community in teaching and leadership positions, and child-directed learning in the form of child choice and play. K–2 programs have strengths in teacher-directed instruction, training in how to teach reading, individualizing instruction according to academic needs and strengths, and the value of progress monitoring for future achievement.

A concrete example of lack of continuity between EB children's PreK and kindergarten experience follows. A Head Start program established alphabet knowledge as a priority. In the spring, children knew, on average, 17 uppercase letter names and

13 uppercase letter sounds. Yet, in kindergarten, all children began the year learning all the letters all over again.

Admittedly, establishing continuity across PreK–2 in language and literacy programs is an endeavor to be accomplished over several years. A significant initial challenge is figuring out ways that PreK and K–2 teachers can be brought into contact amid scheduling and other structural challenges. Consider the suggestions shown in Figure 1.3.

> ***Apply Your Knowledge:*** Write a brief bulleted letter to (1) a publisher or sales representative of a language or literacy program used in your classroom, or (2) a principal or literacy or ELD specialist. Identify a few of the benefits of PreK-2 continuity and how each individual could support language and literacy achievement of EB children. This exercise is one where the role of an advocate for EBs is called upon.

ALLIANCES WITH FAMILIES FOR LANGUAGE AND LITERACY SUCCESS

Children's families are their first teachers. Parents, grandparents, other family members, domestic partners, and foster parents are among those who may have the primary responsibility for taking care of young EBs. This diversity among those privileged with caring for and teaching young EBs is important to be keenly aware of and sensitive to in creating alliances for language and literacy success with families. For example, sending home a letter addressed to "parents" can signal to less traditional families that their unique family constellation is not recognized by educators. I purposefully selected the term *creating alliances* to capture the mutually shared purpose, teamwork, and two-way interaction that form the bedrock for family engagement practices with the most promise for contributing to language and literacy success. Within an alliance, both educators and families share responsibility for the success of home and classroom collaborative efforts.

The traditional term *family involvement* has tended to be based on the view that the proper role of families is to support and comply with the one-way requests made by schools. These requests and expectations are well motivated and reflect the professional competence of educators to make recommendations for ensuring academic achievement. However, new visions of family-school relationships are needed to marshal the significant help that families can provide.

Research suggests school-family programs most likely to lead to children's language and literacy success have the following characteristics:

- They convey to families a genuine interest in and knowledge of their child.
- They enact practices that specifically target language and literacy learning.

Figure 1.3. First-Step Possibilities for Establishing Language and Literacy Continuity Between PreK and K–2

- Advocate with school, program, and district leaders for resources to develop PreK–2 continuities.
- Determine procedures that will allow PreK and K–2 teachers to get together on a regular basis.
- Formally share, explain, and examine language and literacy materials used by each program.
- Establish the overlap in and distinctions between the PreK language and literacy standards and those of the K–2 programs.
- Learn how families are involved in each program.
- Share major instructional practices used for teaching language and literacy.
- Collaboratively determine one limited domain to focus on (such as vocabulary, alphabet learning, or family collaboration) and begin to develop a PreK–2 continuum for that domain.

- They provide families with help and practice in how to use language with their children in ways likely to lead to language and cognitive growth.
- They establish two-way communication that is responsive to families' priorities, preferences, and needs.

One particularly important and unique way that families can support their children's language and literacy success will be through the utilization of their competence with children's first language. A second key way that families can contribute to their children's language and literacy success is by activating, drawing upon, and growing familial, cultural, and personal Wellsprings of Promise in ways likely to support language and literacy success. Helping families obtain knowledge and resources to enable them to capitalize upon these strengths in the home and community is a necessary component of family-school alliances for EBs' language and literacy success.

There are parallels between classrooms and homes in the overarching frameworks that will lead to language and literacy accomplishment. A first parallel is that in homes, as in classrooms, language and literacy growth is nurtured when there is a clear focus on cognitive stimulation, coupled with positive emotional relationships that increase children's sense of security, well-being, and emotional connectedness. The second parallel is that family members who have a significant role in children's learning, like teachers, need support in how to provide the most effective help to children. An essential part of this support is to position the whole endeavor within the idea of creating an alliance with families that takes into account cultural characteristics, belief systems, and the personal experiences and needs of family members themselves. Helpfulness and encouragement are key dispositions for creating an alliance with families. Thinking of each contact with families as an opportunity for finding out and listening as well as for showing and talking is an important frame of mind.

Families are eager, although sometimes wary and uncertain, to create alliances with educators. Families understand deeply that learning English is a gateway for economic security and that their children's day-to-day positive experiences in school are important for their happiness and well-being. As you develop some ideas for creating an alliance with families of emergent bilinguals in your classroom, doing the following, every time, will help launch efforts that can be rewarding to families and educators and, most important, can support children's language and literacy success:

- Discuss your idea with families and/or other community members and solicit their input on how to implement, modify, and/or change the idea.
- Determine how you are going to create the circumstances for the alliance to occur (after-school meeting, communication with outreach personnel, parent network, flyer).
- Identify the language and literacy benefits that could be acquired.
- List the materials and knowledge supports that families may need to be able to enact the recommended practices.
- Enlist bilingual or community-involved family members to explain and promote the planned program/practices.
- Start small, with one or two well-planned, specific programs/practices. Implement these and obtain family feedback for solving problems and improving, and stick with the practice long enough to get results.
- Explicitly connect home experiences with those in the classroom

Chapters 2–8 contain specific recommendations for creating family alliances tied to the content in each chapter. Successful implementation of these recommendations will take a significant amount of thought and planning, but the gains for the EBs in your classroom will be worth the effort.

CONNECTIONS TO THE COMMON CORE STATE STANDARDS AND PRESCHOOL LEARNING STANDARDS

To effectively and gracefully achieve the high levels of academic competence specified in the Common Core State Standards for English Language Arts and PreK language and literacy standards and frameworks, EBs need rich language, sophisticated thinking, and deep knowledge about the social, physical, and artistic world (see Figure 1.4).

The Common Core State Standards for English Language Arts (ELA) is a framework for K–12 students that spells out key competencies in speaking, listening, reading, and writing believed to be needed by all children to be career and college ready (National Governors Association Center for Best Practices & Council of Chief State School Officers, 2010). Standards for preschool children are not included. The CCSS standards have been adopted by 42 states and the District of Columbia as of

Figure 1.4. Components Needed to Meet Language and Literacy Standards

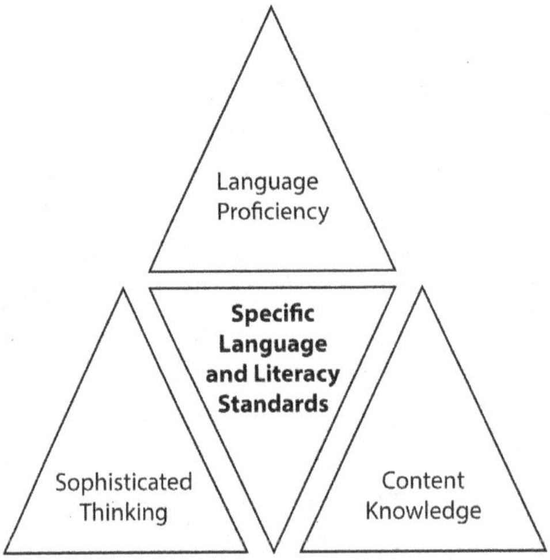

this writing. There has been a swift uptick in the number of states adopting PreK learning standards, guidelines, or frameworks in the past decade. One change from earlier PreK standards and frameworks has been an increased emphasis on literacy and mathematics learning. However, there is substantial variability with respect to the importance assigned to preschool literacy foundations, such as the alphabet and phonological awareness.

In both the CCSS and many PreK standards there is a notable lack of sufficient attention and specificity related to the challenges and instructional supports needed by EBs. The introduction to the CCSS states that identifying the needs of EBs is "beyond the scope of the Standards." (National Governors Association Center for Best Practices & Council of Chief State School Officers, 2010) A subsequent document posted to the CCSS website (www.corestandards.org) provides a number of very general instructional adaptations to help EBs achieve the CCSS for ELA. The supports listed for EBs are a good start, but they don't have sufficient detail on how to accomplish the recommended adaptations, as shown in the following:

- Instructional supports to make grade-level material comprehensible
- Modified assessments
- Additional time to complete grade-level standards
- Classroom interaction to develop concepts and disciplinary academic language
- Interaction with proficient English speakers
- Qualified teachers who use practices that improve achievement

Within the general PreK guidelines, fewer than half of the states have separate guidelines or sections specifically addressing EBs (Head Start, n.d.).

In each chapter within this book, I provide explanations and guidance on practices for teaching EBs to capitalize on the opportunities, overcome the challenges, and supplement the omissions within both the CCSS and preschool standards. Figure 1.5 summarizes the major strengths, challenges, and omissions of the CCSS and preschool foundations related to EBs. Please take some time to study it.

> *Apply Your Knowledge:* Based on your experience with PreK standards or the CCSS, are there other positive emphases, challenges, or omissions to include in Figure 1.5? You might want to pencil them in on the chart.

Benefits of Standards

Both current PreK standards and K–2 CCSS identify child outcomes dictating changes in curriculum and instructional practices that can be of real benefit to EBs. These child outcomes include stronger emphases on language production, vocabulary knowledge, knowledge of language structure, and competence with both narrative and informational text. The emphasis on language production within PreK–2 standards should lead to proactive practices to engage young EBs in English production early in the second language acquisition process. Both sets of standards emphasize conceptual knowledge and high-level thinking. This emphasis has the potential to lead to increased curricular and instructional support for EBs in these areas. However, achieving these competencies will be very challenging for EBs, with the challenge commensurate with EB children's level of English proficiency.

Concerns Related to Standards

The most significant omission in the two sets of standards is a strong endorsement for using children's first language in classrooms for instruction and learning. Though preschool foundations strongly acknowledge the value and importance of first languages, the presence of PreK bilingual and dual-immersion programs or extensive use of first language in classrooms is limited. Head Start is making extensive efforts to develop an integrated set of principles and practices related to first language. This effort includes making materials available in a number of languages. Head Start's planned language program can be reviewed at https://eclkc.ohs.acf.hhs.gov/hslc/tta-system/cultural-linguistic/planned-language-approach/home-language.html. If you are a K–2 teacher, compare this to the program that has been articulated regarding first language in your district. How do the two compare?

Another concern with the CCSS and PreK standards is that they do not recommend the types of instruction to be used to achieve standards. The CCSS encourage teachers to develop their own instructional materials, select their own texts, and teach in the manner they feel is most suitable for their students. PreK standards

Figure 1.5. What's Most Pertinent for EBs: Preschool Foundations and Common Core State Standards

Feature	Preschool Foundations	Common Core State Standards
Positive Emphases	Language focus Language production Language interaction Vocabulary Literacy precursors Narrative and informational text Positive engagement Value of home language	Language focus Language production Language structure Vocabulary Student collaboration Narrative and informational text
Challenges	Limited time in half-day programs Implementation of small groups for academic learning Teacher instructional experience	Text complexity Close reading Yearly expectations Oral presentations Abstract language used in instruction
Worrisome Omissions	Use of home language Language structure Unambiguous endorsement of explicit, teacher-directed instruction Emphasis on early English usage Detail on effective literacy teaching practices for EBs	Value and use of home language Strong emphasis on learning to read skills Research on best methods of teaching Importance of curriculum Perseverance as an outcome Preschool standards Detail on needs of EBs

are generally quiet on methods of teaching beyond recommendations to incorporate play, choice, learning centers, and intentional teaching. A twofold worry stems from the absence of a strong statement that instruction must be guided by existing evidence in the CCSS and many preschool standards First, research in some areas strongly indicates that certain teaching practices are more effective than others. One example is the value of explicit, teacher-directed instruction for learning reading foundations, comprehension strategies, and vocabulary across the PreK–2 span. The second worry is the amount of effort and time that teachers must spend on developing and selecting materials rather than honing instructional practice. To be sure, teachers should reflect upon and select and modify what and how they teach using principles and knowledge that have been verified with research evidence. But it is a daunting task to plan how and what to teach every day for beginning reading instruction. This worry is amplified by a recent report from *Education Week* that reports the sources of instructional materials teachers are using to teach CCSS (Heitin, 2016). More than 95% of teachers reported extensive use of teacher- or district-selected materials. Fewer than 50% reported using a particular curriculum.

The Wider Educational Landscape

Standards by themselves are only one element of the multifaceted context that will influence EBs' language and literacy achievement. In a chapter I wrote on the Common Core, I stated it this way:

> Standards alone will not determine the academic achievement or underachievement of English learners. They are but one piece of a very complex mosaic of schooling influences on English learners' achievement. These effects include the response of schools to students' cultural, linguistic, and socioeconomic circumstances; the emotional experiences imparted through daily classroom interactions with teachers and peers; the richness of the curriculum; the quality of the instruction; the effectiveness of English language development programs; the degree to which learning opportunities foster engagement, motivation, and self-regulation; the degree to which standards support learning; the decisions made on the basis of progress monitoring; and the practices for meaningful and positive collaborations among educators and families, among others. The aggregate of the day-to-day, lived experience of each English learner during school will tell the tale. (Roberts, 2013, p. 103)

Teachers are striving to secure improvements in EBs' academic achievement within the following contexts:

- Increasing linguistic diversity of children attending PreK–2 educational programs
- Demand for high levels of English language and literacy competence
- Long-term disparities in literacy achievement between many EB children and non-EB children

Educators need the mindset, grit, and instructional tools to begin righting the course of American education for EBs. There is room enough for improvement, evidence enough on how to accomplish improvement, and educator will and public pressure enough to mandate improvement in language and literacy education for EBs. I hope this book can become a stalwart support as you begin or continue to captain your instructional ship toward the destination of language and literacy achievement for all EBs.

Educational Principles in Chapter 1

1. Consistently increase the extent to which school and classroom practices draw upon children's and their families' linguistic, familial, and cultural Wellsprings of Promise.
2. Hold steadfast every day to high expectations and optimism for language and literacy achievement for all emergent bilinguals.
3. Develop comprehensive plans and ongoing focus to help families increase the amount of cognitive stimulation in children's homes.
4. Establish programmatic policy and practices to obtain information on the patterns of L1 and L2 language use in the home.
5. Seek out and support the hiring of teachers who come from a wide range of cultures and language backgrounds.
6. Provide teachers with the knowledge of the English language needed to effectively teach language and literacy and the support needed to develop instructional practices that are most effective for EBs.
7. Establish the development of PreK–2 language and literacy learning continuums as a priority for the language and literacy achievement of EBs.

CHAPTER 2

Incorporating First Language Strength

IMPORTANT RESEARCH FINDINGS ABOUT FIRST LANGUAGE

- Language is intimately intertwined with identity, culture, and thinking.
- Strength in the primary language is a support for English acquisition and achievement.
- Activation of the primary language is an underutilized support for school achievement.
- Emergent bilingual children learn reading foundations and master English in bilingual programs just as well as or better than similar children do in English-only programs.
- The quality of the instruction is the most important factor related to achievement in bilingual programs.
- There is an important distinction between social/functional (communicative) language and academic language.
- Practices for activating the first language (L1) can be utilized in all PreK–2 classrooms.

As explained in Chapter 1, emergent bilinguals (EBs) bring many resources to the classroom. These resources can be represented by the three nested circles portraying a child's developmental system, shown in Figure 2.1.

The innermost of the three circles represents the inner resources of children. These resources include their language, knowledge of the world, emotional well-being, thinking processes, self-identity, and motivation to master their environment. The next circle surrounding the central self-system is the family, community, and cultural influences on development that typically bestow resources on children. Their family caregivers love them, teach them, and want them to learn English (L2) and to succeed in school (Ngo & Lee, 2007; Roberts, 2008). Cultural and community experiences provide children with spiritual beliefs, values, and practices imbued with historical, political, and social meaningfulness (Caplan, Chou, & Whitmore, 1991). These resources help children construct a unique sense of self and become embedded within a cultural framework that broadens and deepens their sense of who they are. The resources associated with these first two circles within the developmental system have been developing from infancy.

Figure 2.1. Influences on a Child's Developmental System

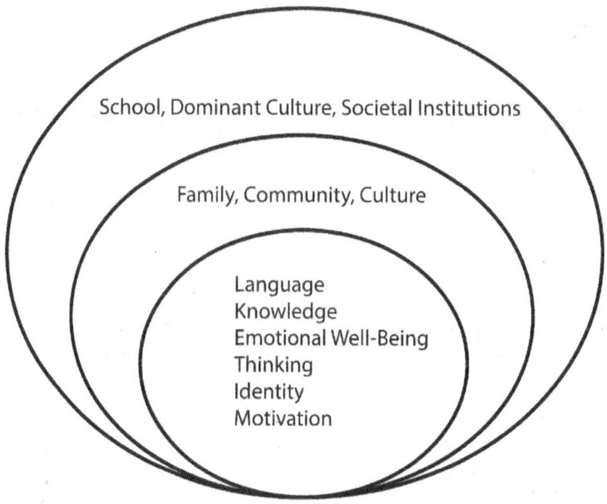

The third and outermost circle of the developmental system includes influences further from the child's immediate life and are less personal. These include societal influences and institutions such as schooling. All of these systems interact in multiple and complex ways. Language is deeply embedded within all of these interactions. When these systems interact compatibly, development is smoothed. You might think of it like the circles that naturally and beautifully emanate from a central pebble thrown into a pool of water. When the sources of influence on a child's development represented in the three circles clash or present significant disruptions, development must adjust and recalibrate. Children whose first language is English, who are not socioeconomically at risk, and whose familial, cultural, and community experiences are more similar to those they will encounter in school are positioned to experience a developmental niche in school classrooms that is largely an extension of their early development. This fit establishes a foundation for school achievement. For English learners whose language, experience, and family and cultural socialization are less aligned with practices in schools, and sometimes may even conflict with them, the adjustment is more challenging. These challenges may detract from and interfere with achievement. In this chapter the nature of children's connection to their first language and the social and cognitive benefits of knowing two or more languages is explained. The benefits to school-family alliances that can accrue from using the home language in classrooms are described. Schoolwide programs and classroom practices to eliminate barriers for using children's first languages, and to activate and utilize first languages for English language and literacy achievement in a variety of classroom settings, are presented.

WHY UTILIZE EMERGENT BILINGUALS' FIRST LANGUAGE IN THE CLASSROOM?

Children's Deep Connection to Their First Language

Educational Principle 1: Explicitly consider how children's first language relates to each programmatic decision that is made.

Children's primary language is intimately intertwined with their personal and cultural identity, their cognitive knowledge and thinking processes, and the important relationships they have established. A positive response from schools to the very personal cognitive and social–emotional connections EBs have with their first language is a critical condition for school achievement. It is important in educational planning, all the time and every time, to keep at the forefront an understanding of the social–emotional as well as cognitive purposes for which children have used their first language, with an eye to establishing continuity between those purposes and school experience, while augmenting prior experiences with new language and ways of being. Integration of language, social and emotional development, and cognitive development characterizes all humans, including English learners and English fluent (EF) children.

Emergent bilingual children have developed strength in their first language prior to entering English-dominant schools. Across the PreK–2 developmental period, children can use their typically well-developed first languages to effectively communicate their wants and needs, establish and negotiate relationships, participate in cultural and community practices, think and reason, capture and express their world experience, and creatively and imaginatively manipulate language. These competencies provide a positive social–emotional and cognitive foundation for acquisition of a second language and for academic learning.

Apply Your Knowledge: List the names of the EB children in your classroom on a sheet with eight columns. These columns will be used to inventory first language resources of your students.Label the columns "Number of people in the household literate in first language," "Parents completed 8 or more years of schooling," "Lives in community where L1 is richly spoken," "Frequent storybook reading or oral storytelling in first language," "Attends L1 school," "Has extended family members who speak L1," and "Number of older siblings who speak English." It may be challenging to find out some of this information. The more "yes" answers or checks you have for each child will indicate the likelihood of stronger first language resources.

Teaching Practice 1: Incorporate meaningful and regular use of children's first language in the classroom for both social-emotional and academic/cognitive purposes.

Affirmation of children's first language competencies by teachers and other educators communicates to children and their families that they contribute language resources valuable for school learning (Cummins, 2000). Figure 2.2 provides many suggestions for how teachers can encourage families to strengthen their emergent bilingual children's first language. Utilization of first language competencies in classrooms demonstrates this affirmation strongly and concretely. Even preschool children are sensitive to classroom language choices. I have conducted research in settings with a large Hmong-speaking population and no Hmong-capable teaching staff. In one preschool I recruited a Hmong-speaking teaching assistant. I was present in the classroom when she introduced herself, first in English and then in Hmong. Almost immediately after she spoke Hmong, many Hmong-speaking children began to smile, giggle, and even roll around on the carpet. At the age of 4, they found it very noteworthy that a teacher was speaking Hmong.

Failing to utilize children's first language in classroom settings and focusing on EBs' limited English proficiency overlooks children's first language strength, communicates to families that they have little to offer for school success, and carries increased risk that the teacher will view children as linguistically limited. This may be followed by lowered teacher expectations, and messages and practices that create barriers for families to connect with schools. These conditions are school-based factors that contribute to the achievement challenges experienced by English learners (Auerbach, 2010).

> *Apply Your Knowledge:* Imagine you are an anthropologist studying language development. Select one of the EB children in your classroom to study for 1 week. Observe this child in the classroom with peers and when doing independent work. Observe her while she is having a meal and while she is outside on the playground. Watch her when she is with her family before and after school. Try to find someone who speaks the child's language (maybe you) to tell you what they have observed about the extent and quality of the child's L1. Identify the practices in your classroom that support or use this child's first language. With what you learned from this study, plan three new practices that you can actually do. Start on one tomorrow.

The Benefits of Knowing Two Languages

Educational Principle 2: Establish maintenance and development of their first language as an explicit educational goal for all emergent bilingual children.

Figure 2.2. How to Engage Families in Strengthening Their Emergent Bilingual Children's First Language

- Regularly recommend and explain to families why they should use the language they and their child can communicate best in at home.
- Help families to enact the following practices when talking with their children:
  - » Be nice when talking.
  - » Just talk and use words children don't know; use many different words for the same idea or thing.
  - » Listen to what children say and show this by responding to them.
  - » Tell children about home and community activities of daily living, events, and activities.
  - » Allow children to choose topics of conversation and to switch to new things to talk about.
- Help families learn how to sit together and look at children's storybooks and informational books and talk together about the pictures in the first language, and help them understand why this practice is valuable.
- Encourage families to talk together about family artifacts such as photos and mementos using the first language.
- Ask families to retell and remember recent events such as a trip to the park or grocery store or a religious service in the first language, sharing the talk with their children.
- Ask families to retell movies and TV shows, sharing the talk with their children.
- Ask families to label items in the home in their first language; children can add the English words as they learn them.
- Help families talk together with children in their first language about "what if" imaginary events and upcoming family activities.
- Ask families to write down children's descriptions, questions, and stories about artifacts and experiences in the home and community, send them to school, and then post them in the classroom.
- Provide website addresses for translator programs and first language resources (books, family guides to social services, and so forth).
- Record children's singing, storytelling, book or picture reading, talking with family members, and so on. Let children listen to the recordings and ask questions that get children to talk more, such as "What do you think of that?" "What other songs could you sing?" "Can you explain to me what you said?"
- Suggest that families talk together playfully during car rides, trips to the grocery, mealtimes, bathing and nighttime routines, watching a sports game, and so on.
- Provide parents with conversation starters in the first language on topics related to classroom units of study.
- Provide specific vocabulary words in the first language related to units of study. Ask families to talk about these words together with their child.
- Plan a few ways across several grade levels for family members to use their first language in the classroom with small groups of one to three children and teach volunteer family members how to carry out the practice in the classroom (for example, talk about picture books, write down children's telling of their personal experiences, and so forth).
- Encourage families to take pictures in their homes and communities and talk together with children about them, and then send the pictures to school for further use in classroom L1 or L2 activities.

Knowing two languages benefits social–emotional well-being, first and second language competencies, and thinking (cognitive) processes. Let's examine these benefits in more detail.

Children use their first language to navigate, organize, remember, and act on their social and physical environments. A language shared between children and their families strengthens emotional bonds. These bonds are a resource for navigating the increasing social, emotional, and cognitive complexity that accompanies development. The initial structure of children's personal identity is also connected with their first language. It is the language they have used to learn, and to express their desires, preferences, reactions, unique experiences, and joy and confidence with language. It is the language in which they first heard "I love you" or celebrated their First Communion. It is the language they have used as they develop their cultural and family roles as a member of a particular faith, cultural group, and as a son, daughter, brother, or sister. EB children with a strong L1 have stronger identity formation and self-esteem compared with children who are fluent in their L2 (English), but are not fluent in L1 (Portes & Hao, 2002).

There are two major ways in which knowing more than one language benefits language competence. Bilingualism increases children's flexible use of language and may sharpen their awareness of language as a system. This awareness is revealed when for example, Damien, a student, explains that "A word is used to name something," and confidently agrees that "We could call a flower a *flasmon* if everyone agreed to do it." These language skills are called *metalinguistic awareness*. Experience with more than one language may also foster more advanced ability to analyze grammar and word forms, such as detecting that there is something wrong with the sentence "He hopping up the street."

How might knowing more than one language lead to these language benefits? As children learn a second language, they subconsciously, or implicitly, experience extensive opportunities to compare and contrast two language systems. In so doing, concepts about the nature of language bubble to the top, enabling children to think about what a word is or how language refers to real things.

There is more good news associated with knowing two languages, in the form of cognitive, or thinking, benefits. Heightened capacity to control one's thinking accrues from knowing two languages (Poarch & Bialystok, 2015). This control includes, for example, the ability to flexibly shift attention from the daily calendar to the introduction of a new book, and to multitask. The suite of skills involved in controlling thinking is called *executive function*. This executive function advantage is reliably seen even in EB infants and, thus, emerges with only a bit of second language exposure. The thinking advantage becomes larger as tasks become more difficult (Raluca, Bialystok, Castro, & Sanchez, 2014). When children can control their thinking, they can better control themselves—*self-regulate*—a desired outcome in many preschool learning standards.

Incorporating first language use into school settings develops the first language and thereby the social–emotional, learning, and thinking benefits it can provide.

These social–emotional and cognitive benefits are useful in classroom language and literacy learning.

> *Apply Your Knowledge:* Request to have ongoing planning time devoted to the topic of increasing classroom first language usage in your team, grade-level, or site meetings. Make the same request for professional development. Ask for first language support from coaches or EB language support personnel.

First Language Competence and English Language Arts Achievement

There is a cooperative relationship between EBs' strong first language and literacy and their success in acquiring strong second language and literacy in PreK–2 (August & Hakuta, 1997; Slavin & Cheung, 2005; Winsler, Kim, & Richard, 2014). Teachers can be confident that children's L1 and L2 work together, although there will be influences and carryover from one language to another. This cooperation is consistent with the research on brain function in EBs showing that both languages are working during all language activity. One of the most prevalent myths believed by the public and some teachers is that teaching L1 reading and language arts impedes or interferes with L2 reading and English language arts. Recent policy and legislation in several states establishing English-only education of EBs is partially based on this myth. Though it may seem logical to suppose that time spent with L1 takes away time for learning L2 and thus interferes with L2 achievement, the research indicates otherwise (August & Hakuta, 1997; Genesee, Lindholm-Leary, Saunders, & Christian, 2006; Rolstad, Mahoney, & Glass, 2005).

L1 competencies can be drawn upon in L2 learning. First language vocabulary knowledge, comprehension strategies, language skills needed in phonological awareness and phonics, and conceptual knowledge stored in the brain in the first language (Genesee et al., 2006) can all be transferred to L2 language and literacy learning. However, the availability of first language resources (1) does not occur automatically, (2) is more likely to occur in languages that are more similar to English, and (3) is harder to activate for preschool than for grade 2 children (Branum-Martin, Foorman, Francis, & Mehta, 2010). It is very difficult for a teacher to provide direct instruction in how and when to activate and apply the skills from the first language to the second. I recommend grouping children who share the same L1 in pairs or small groups to talk and work together using L1 within English lessons, particularly on topics where children's prior knowledge might be applicable. A science unit on plant growth would be such a topic. And remember that L1 interaction will be helpful for L2 learning and achievement.

Teaching Practice 2: Include in English lessons routines for EBs to use L1 to discuss new English vocabulary, share text-related background knowledge, and practice phonological awareness activities with other EBs who speak the same first language.

A study I conducted with preschool EBs showed how the first and second language can work together (Roberts, 2008). Families were given classic storybooks in English or their first language for home reading. Classroom book reading and vocabulary instruction in English followed. Preschool EBs were just as successful in acquiring English storybook vocabulary from classroom instruction when they read the books at home in L1 as when they read books at home in English. There was some evidence that the storybooks in the first language may have been most useful for English vocabulary growth. Children's first language is a reservoir and song of self, relationship, experience, and thinking processes. You can help children sing their first language song fully, with gusto, and regularly in your classroom.

Teaching Practice 3: Encourage and help families to use the language they know best for social/functional and academic purposes at home.

HOW TO STRENGTHEN EMEGENT BILINGUALS' FIRST LANGUAGE IN THE CLASSROOM

Programs to Achieve Bilingualism

Educational Principle 3: Advocate for and support the development of high-quality bilingual education programs.
Educational Principle 4: Establish PreK–2 partnerships to develop comprehensive bilingual programs that last a minimum of 4 years.

Four reviews conducted over the past 30 years of the highest-quality research on educating EBs all concluded that EBs attending programs with dual-language instruction (instruction in both children's first language and English) learn English at least as well as EBs in English-only programs (Greene, 1997: Rolstad, Mahoney, & Glass, 2005; Slavin & Cheung, 2005; Willig, 1985). They also, of course, score higher on tests of L1. For example, López and Tashakkori (2006) found that kindergarten and grade 1 EB children in a dual-immersion program achieved as well as children in a program that did not include L1 and, remarkably, reached the level of English oral proficiency to exit L2 support services more quickly. Other studies not included in the reviews have reported the same basic findings for preschool EBs (e.g., Barnett, Yarosz, Thomas, Jung, & Blanco, 2007; Burchinal et al., 2012). The PreK–2 research findings go against the conjecture that EBs in English-only programs have higher achievement in English (Kim, Hutchison, & Winsler, 2013).

Preschool programs have long been encouraged to support children's first language (e.g., National Association for the Education of Young Children, 1995).

This encouragement has not led to widespread bilingual education programs for preschool children, but it has created a positive disposition toward cultural and linguistic diversity that can encourage teachers, program leaders, and the community toward program practices moving toward the bilingual ideal. For kindergarten through grade 2 and beyond, recent years have seen an increase in legislation specifically curtailing bilingual programs, and a resulting demise in such programs (Pufahl & Rhodes, 2011). There is some indication that motivated teachers, other educators, and families are contributing to a small resurgence in bilingual programs, particularly two-way or dual-immersion (English and L1) programs. For example, in the metropolitan area where I live, there are currently dual-immersion programs in English-Cantonese, English-Hmong, and English-Spanish. These programs were initiated through the County Office of Education and took life in the state of California, which has legislation significantly curtailing bilingual education although new initiatives supporting it has been passed. So there is hope and possibility.

Cummins (2000) argues that the fundamental criterion for a program to effectively develop both the first language and English is that the goal must be for children to become bilingual. Within bilingual programs, the quality of the instruction is the most important factor determining reading and language arts achievement (Slavin & Cheung, 2005). The necessary components of an effective bilingual program are identified in Figure 2.3. The details of how much each language is used each year, which language is used first, and which language is used for which subject or activity can be variable, providing flexibility based on the available resources, needs, and constraints. For example, limited availability of bilingual teachers could be addressed with a team-teaching approach where a bilingual teacher provides first language instruction and the English-only teacher provides English instruction. Children might learn to read in L1 or L2.

Early childhood teachers are likely to feel pressure for children to demonstrate English proficiency quickly. However, it will take 4 to 7 years for EBs in bilingual programs to become truly bilingual. Documented progress in each language for each child is a necessary part of progress monitoring to assure teachers and those responsible for accountability that the bilingual program is working. Remember, there is no good evidence to think that abandoning the first language and providing equal-quality, English-only instruction will achieve the goal of truly bilingual children any better or any faster. Good work takes time.

> ***Apply Your Knowledge:*** Write a letter to a site administrator or community leader recommending to them that they establish a bilingual preschool program. Base your letter on information from this chapter. Include information on the social-emotional (personal and social identity, valuing diversity, family communication) and cognitive (primary language, second language and literacy, language awareness, academic language) benefits.

Figure 2.3. Characteristics of Effective Bilingual Programs

Goal: Bilingualism—speaking, reading, and writing proficiency in both languages

Sufficient duration: 4 (minimum)–7 years

Organizational plan:

- Details on the sequencing of language used for reading, writing, speaking, listening, and subject areas
- Plan can be explained by all school personnel and the community
- Practices to affirm children's personal, family, and cultural identity
- Professional development addressing L1 and L2 development and teaching practices for EBs
- Strong family collaboration plan

Human resources:

- All stakeholders committed to the goal of bilingualism
- Certified bilingual teachers
- Monolingual English teachers
- Bilingual and monolingual teaching assistants
- Family and community members
- Directors and principals who function as committed leaders

Material resources:

- Teaching and learning materials for speaking, listening, reading, and writing in both languages
- A written description of the program that can be explained by those using it
- Curriculum that represents experiences and values of participating children

Using First Language in English-Instruction Dominant Classrooms

Educational Principle 5: Advocate for and support the hiring of teachers and other school personnel who have proficiency in more than one language, particularly those languages that are represented in your classroom and school.

Some of you may have been thinking: "There are too many different languages in my classroom for a bilingual program to be possible"; "There are no materials or certified teachers in many of the languages I work with"; "I live in a state or district where bilingual programs are prohibited"; or "I speak only English." These are very real circumstances that may, at the moment, limit the availability of bilingual programs. Yet classroom methods for activating first languages and richly incorporating them to help EB children access the English curriculum and to master the CCSS and preschool learning standards are still very possible. As the saying goes, "Where there is a will, there is a way."

One of the first teaching practices to develop is a cue, method, or routine to signal children when they should use L1 or L2. It is easier for a teacher to guide this if he shares an L1 with EBs because children will usually follow the teacher's lead in which language to use (Chang et al., 2007; Chesterfield, Chesterfield, Hayes-Latimer, & Chavez, 1983). In one of my research studies, we could not figure out how to get 4-year-old children to use Hmong in the classroom. We eventually had some success by having a Hmong parent speak Hmong, accompanied by a signal of raising one finger. We had a teacher standing in the exact same spot speak English accompanied by raising two fingers. With some practice, we were pretty successful in having children switch languages using the one- or two-finger signal. If all teachers in your school are regularly activating first language with an effective cue, children will become adept at switching.

Teaching Practice 4: Develop a method to efficiently signal to children when they are expected to use their first language and when they are expected to use English.

Decisions on when to activate children's first language should be made based on the goal of each lesson and an "English difficulty gradient," as shown in Figure 2.4. When the language of instruction and the content to be learned are both English, such as English language development or the spellings of English words, children should mostly use English. In contrast, when the instruction will be provided in English but the content to be learned is concepts, such as the process of metamorphosis or a demanding thinking process such as supporting an argument with evidence from the text, then activating the first language could be desirable. Both of these examples feature academic learning. Demonstrations, translation, and direct teaching to ensure children understand the meaning of the key words such as *metamorphosis* and *evidence* are necessary. Studies have suggested that the first language tends to be used in classrooms for functional and social–emotional purposes, while English is used for more academic purposes. The use of the first language for social relationships and classroom daily life is important. However, activating the first language during academic learning is very important for L1 development and for enabling L1 learning to transfer to L2 achievement.

Teaching Practice 5: Let the goal of each lesson inform when to activate children's first language.

The *English difficulty gradient* (see Figure 2.4) provides guidance on when the first language may be most beneficial. The following example will show you how you can use it: Imagine your 2nd-grade class has just completed reading an informational history text related to George Washington crossing the Delaware. Your learning goal, consistent with the CCSS, is for children to use details from the text as evidence. You

Figure 2.4. English Difficulty Gradient

Contains Less	⟵ Learning Activity ⟶	Contains More
	Speeded responses and fast pacing required Novel/unfamiliar learning Complex or difficult ideas or procedures/difficulty Ideas must be generated by students generation Learning is not supported by context; children must learn from language only Number of steps in directions or process	
Activity is Easier	English required	Activity is Harder

plan for children to brainstorm ideas for alternatives for crossing the river and to have them identify details from the text (time of day, weather, terrain, and so on) to support plausible options. You will have a discussion of "evidence" at the close of the lesson. This brainstorming activity is one that requires children to generate ideas, involves a multistep process, and in which the concept of "evidence" is fairly sophisticated. The English difficulty gradient figure indicates that when learning activities require student to generate ideas, use a multistep process and contains sophisticated ideas using English, it is harder (bottom of figure) and therefore use of L1 would be very useful during this learning activity.

Activating L1 for small-group/partner brainstorming with other L1 speakers could be used, initially followed by children stating in English within their group what they believe is the best alternative. Groups of same-language partners can be of varying sizes; there may be four Spanish speakers in each of two groups, one pair that speaks Urdu, and an additional three groups of English fluent children. Children without a language partner will work together with teacher support. Forming these groupings can and should become routine and should happen very quickly. You may worry that you cannot monitor children's on-task behavior if they are speaking in a different language. The best remedy for this worry is having strong relationships with students, coupled with interesting topics and engaging activities.

In addition to directly activating L1 during instruction, with persistence and creativity you can enlist other L1 helpers into the classroom. Buddy programs with older children who are fluent in L1 can help explain and practice English learning activities. If they are literate, they could read L1 storybooks. One of the best activities I have seen for L1 family helpers in classrooms is to record children's narratives of their personal experiences (see Figure 2.5).

Teaching Practice 6: Consider the English difficulty gradient when deciding when to activate children's first language.
Teaching Practice 7: Group together children who speak the same language for some language and literacy learning.

Figure 2.5. Example of Systematically Orchestrating the First Language and English

I developed a bilingual toolkit to provide L1 instruction aligned with each thematic unit of a preschool literacy curriculum. Bilingual teaching assistants explained important concepts and vocabulary for the unit in L1 and then introduced the related English word. Retelling of stories that went with each unit using pictures was conducted in L1. Lessons were delivered to small groups of three to six students, which elicited high levels of participation from EB children. Every day, each lesson had the same format so that assistant teachers and children could benefit from the routinized instruction.

Apply Your Knowledge: Go on a first language resource treasure hunt. Begin by listing the languages of children in your classroom for which you need to identify resources.

- Are there staff at your school who have dual-language competencies?
- Are there family members that might provide first language resources in the classroom? What might they be capable of?
- Are there any cultural or community organizations such as libraries that might have materials?
- Are there any first language materials in shops, markets, or health clinics in the community?
- Are there any social service or nonprofit organizations that might provide materials?
- Can money be used to purchase first language literacy materials?
- Investigate online transition programs or apps that you might be able to use right in the classroom.
- What are additional ways to locate both human and material first language resources?

THE PREK–GRADE 2 CONTINUUM: ACTIVATING THE FIRST LANGUAGE

The majority of English language learners in the United States enter preschool or kindergarten (if they have not attended preschool) classrooms speaking only their first language or with their first language proficiency far in advance of their English proficiency. However, there will be substantial variability in the level of development of the first language. As pointed out in Chapter 1, approximately 66% of EBs entering public schools reside in families earning less than 200% of the federal poverty level (EPE Research Center, 2009). Low family socioeconomic status (SES) is a risk factor for L1 language development. Studies have confirmed below-average L1 proficiency in EB children from low-SES families. The level of L1 proficiency in PreK–2 is dependent on both the quantity and quality of the first language to which children have been exposed, primarily within their homes. Some children may attend first language schools, and if they are a recent immigrant, in 1st or 2nd grade they may have a beginning level of L1 literacy. These latter two characteristics are associated with stronger L1.

Children who enter English-dominant schools for the first time at grade 1 or 2 will typically have developed their first language more extensively than children who first enter at preschool. Concerns have been raised about the fate of the first language when children enter English-dominant schools at a young age. There are reports of both L1 loss and L1 preservation. These concerns are well founded because much is at stake. The good news is that appropriate school practices, such as those recommended in this chapter, can foster L1 preservation.

From the onset of first language acquisition, children will be learning words and their meanings (semantics), how words are correctly strung together and modified (syntax/ morphology), and the individual sounds within words (phonology). Children also learn the expectations and rules that guide how, when, where, and to whom they are to speak and with whom they are to interact (pragmatics). These are the manners of language, if you will, and include the following:

- How do you speak to parents?
- Who has the right to verbally tease another?
- Who can start and end conversations?
- What conventions show politeness and interest?
- How are conversations and turn-taking expected to proceed?

These norms will definitely influence children's linguistic and social behavior in classrooms.

To illustrate these ideas, think back to the lesson on Washington crossing the Delaware River. Children were to brainstorm and then individually state their view of the most plausible alternatives for crossing the river. Turn-taking conventions during brainstorming, comfort in giving one's ideas and evaluating the ideas of another, and the inclination to set oneself off from the group are sociocultural variations that may influence how children participate during this lesson. Children from mainstream, middle-class families are more likely to have learned how to use language in the same ways that schools have traditionally rewarded, such as the language practices expected during this lesson. Finding out about your students' sociocultural conversational variations can take some sleuthing. But this sleuthing can pay off because it can lead to adapting lessons to mirror these variations or, alternatively, may alert you to times when children may need extra support and explanation in order to use language in ways that are less familiar to them. There is research showing achievement gains when classroom patterns of language use match the way children use language at home.

Teaching Practice 8: Observe how families, children, peers and other children use language together, and incorporate ways of using language in instruction that are familiar to emergent bilingual children.

Teaching Practice 9: When using language in ways that are less familiar to children, explain what is expected, demonstrate the practice, and allow time for children to learn it.

CONNECTIONS TO THE COMMON CORE STATE STANDARDS AND PRESCHOOL LEARNING STANDARDS

As pointed out in Chapter 1, the CCSS do not affirm the value of, maintenance of, and incorporation of first language strength (Roberts, 2013). National and state preschool learning standards typically identify and respect the value of a first language, but do not stipulate robust practices that are likely to lead to its utilization for social and academic learning. Consequently, an important asset for helping EB children to master PreK–2 standards is not capitalized upon.

The language competencies promoted by knowing two languages can be applied to help children master preschool learning standards and the CCSS. Emergent bilingual children's strength in awareness of language as a system may help them learn reading foundations (alphabet, phonemic awareness, decoding) because they require attention to language structure. The bilingual benefit of sharpened ability to analyze grammar and word forms has direct utility for mastering the Common Core State Standards on language structure. Strengths in multitasking and flexible use of attention that arise from knowing two languages may be one reason why collaborative learning helps EBs. The emphasis on collaboration within the CCSS is an opportunity to support the achievement of EBs. The potential advantage of being bilingual may directly help preschool EBs master self-regulation, a social–emotional learning standard frequently identified.

Apply Your Knowledge: Imagine that you teach 2nd grade. Your grade-level team is concerned about the quality of children's writing in relationship to the CCSS: "Write opinion pieces in which they introduce the topic or book they are writing about, state an opinion, supply reasons that support the opinion, use linking words (e.g., because, and, also) to connect opinion and reasons, and provide a concluding statement." How might the L1 of students be relevant? Here are a few questions to get you started:

- Can any children in my class write in their first language?
- How can I find out which topics I can select that my students know about and are interested in?
- Are the children having difficulty understanding the words *because, and,* and *also*?
- How might I cleverly demonstrate or explain these words so EBs can understand them without complex and abstract verbal definitions?

Supporting children and their families in the development of academic language in L1 is a powerful means of helping EBs master the preschool learning standards and the CCSS. Academic language conforms more to formal grammar rules, and contains specialized vocabulary and concepts related to subjects such as math and science. Enriching children's academic language experiences in L1 at home will walk right with them through the classroom door. Academic language also requires that children talk about and learn through language by itself—it is decontextualized from immediate concrete experience.

Teaching Practice 10: Provide opportunities to use academic, decontextualized first language by talking about past and future events, imaginary worlds, and content-area topics (math, science, social studies) in children's first language.

Using, maintaining, and enhancing children's first language is important for familial, cultural, personal, emotional, and cognitive reasons. First language can be used effectively in a variety of different programs when the goal of bilingualism is embraced and shared among children, families, the larger community, and schools. Carefully planned bilingual programs of sufficient duration, accompanied by teachers with strong language resources in each language and high-quality instruction and materials, can result in students who are strong in both their first language and in English—they are bilingual. Research conducted over 35 years demonstrates that bilingualism is possible and beneficial for both L1 and L2 competencies. In contexts where bilingual programs are not yet available, there are still many ways to effectively incorporate and draw upon children's first language resources, both at home and in school. These practices will serve to maintain and develop the first language and contribute to the mastery of English preschool foundations and the CCSS and similar local state standards.

Educational Principles From Chapter 2

1. Explicitly consider how children's first language relates to each programmatic decision that is made.
2. Establish maintenance and development of their first language as an explicit educational goal for all emergent bilingual children.
3. Advocate for and support the development of high-quality bilingual education programs.
4. Establish PreK–2 partnerships to develop comprehensive bilingual programs that last a minimum of 4 years.
5. Advocate for and support the hiring of teachers and other school personnel who have proficiency in more than one language, particularly those languages that are represented in your classroom and school.

Teaching Practices From Chapter 2

1. Incorporate meaningful and regular use of children's first language in the classroom for both social-emotional and academic/cognitive purposes.
2. Include in English lessons routines for EBs to use L1 to discuss new English vocabulary, share text-related background knowledge, and practice phonological awareness activities with other EBs who speak the same first language.
3. Encourage and help families to use the language they know best for social/functional and academic purposes at home.
4. Develop a method to efficiently signal to children when they are expected to use their first language and when they are expected to use English.
5. Let the goal of each lesson inform when to activate children's first language.
6. Consider the English difficulty gradient when deciding when to activate children's first language.
7. Group together children who speak the same language for some language and literacy learning.
8. Observe how parents, children, and other children use language together, and incorporate ways of using language in instruction that are familiar to emergent bilingual children.
9. When using language in ways that are less familiar to children, explain what is expected, demonstrate the practice, and allow time for children to learn it.
10. Provide opportunities to use decontextualized first language by talking about past and future events, imaginary worlds, and content-area topics (math, science, social studies) in children's first language.

CHAPTER 3

Strengthening English Proficiency

Important Research Findings About Strengthening English Proficiency

- English language proficiency is a centerpiece of EBs' academic success.
- It takes 4 to 7 years to develop English proficiency to the level necessary for learning from challenging texts, content areas, and classroom instruction.
- Language input, intake, and output are all critical for developing English language proficiency.
- The quality of the English language that children hear is related to English oral proficiency.
- Children's English talking is related to English oral proficiency.
- The most effective language development instruction and learning activity focuses on both correct form and meaning.
- Explicit instruction in the structure of the English language and meaningful practice increase proficiency.
- Collaboration is most effective when it is structured, presents students with new learning, leads to forming solution/s, and provides for time to plan language output.
- Sheltered English instruction programs (English-only) programs are less effective than other types of programs for English language proficiency and literacy achievement.

English language proficiency is a centerpiece of the array of competencies EB children need to master the K–2 CCSS in ELA and preschool language and literacy standards. There is a strong relationship between both first and second language oral competence and English language arts achievement from toddlerhood to the end of 2nd grade. Yet estimates indicate that most EBs have difficulty with English and have proficiency levels below those of children of similar socioeconomic status whose first language is English. The effect of oral language strength extends beyond school achievement to influence children's ability to control their behaviors, to form rewarding social connections to others, and to successfully negotiate the English-speaking everyday world, both inside and outside of school.

Much has been said about the ease with which young children acquire language. The optimism for EBs to achieve English proficiency embedded in this belief is helpful. However, research indicates that learning a second language is a complex and lengthy process. As pointed out earlier, current estimates are that it takes between 4 and 7 years to acquire English proficiency (Hakuta, Butler, & Witt, 2000). The shorter estimate pertains to communicative/everyday English and the longer estimate pertains to the academic language required for language and literacy achievement. The span of time to acquire English proficiency provides a sufficient rationale for continuity in language and literacy programs from PreK through grade 2.

One goal of this chapter is to extract from this complexity the major processes involved in second language acquisition (SLA) that can promote communicative and academic English oral proficiency. Teachers must have a deep and clear understanding of the process of second language acquisition before they can plan and enact the instructional practice, and provide the extensive and sophisticated learning activities that can lead to English language proficiency. Within this chapter you will be asked several times to reflect upon your own language and how you use it. Language models have a powerful effect on second (and first) language acquisition. Teachers are language models. These exercises draw attention to the strengths of your language modeling and help you determine areas you might target for future growth as a language model.

HOW CHILDREN LEARN A SECOND (OR FIRST) LANGUAGE

The amount and quality of the language experiences that occur during second language acquisition are at the heart of proficiency. Emotional warmth and children's perceptions that adults are responding to their language have repeatedly been shown to enhance language acquisition. Smiling, expressing mutual enjoyment, sharing back-and-forth conversation where teachers and children are sewing with the same thread of meaning, and responding to children's questions and observations demonstrate teacher warmth and responsivity. Figure 3.1 captures the major forces of second (or first) language acquisition, which will be described below.

Input

Educational Principle 1: Include teacher personal language development as a centerpiece and valid component of professional development.

There are two features of input that should shine brightly in teachers' minds when they are planning for and providing input that will build children's English proficiency. These two features are the *amount* of input and the *quality* of the input. Both at home and school, the amount of language that children hear and the quality

Figure 3.1. Language Acquisition Process

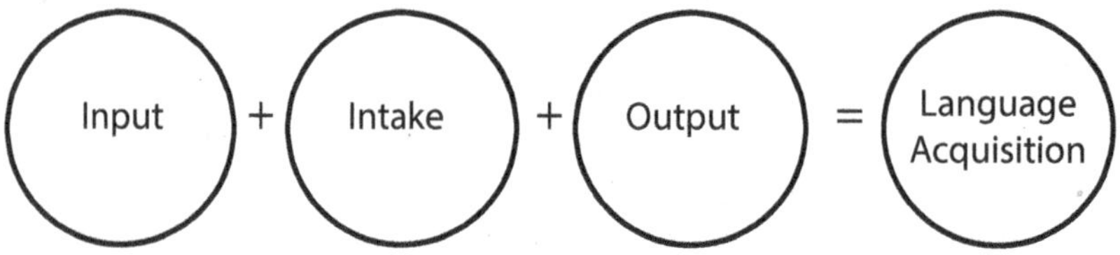

of that language are associated with the level of English proficiency attained (Palermo, Mikulski, Fabes, Hanish, Martin, & Stargel, 2014). Teachers' oral language competence is related to both English and Spanish literacy achievement (Cirino, Pollard-Durodola, Foorman, Carlson, & Francis, 2007).

Although the concept of amount of input is straightforward, you may be wondering, "How do I know that the input I am providing to EBs in my classroom is of high quality?" High-quality input introduces children to more types of words and includes words that are less common synonyms for common words and perhaps includes longer words. For example, changing the word *special* in the sentence "You are a special person" to *unique* or *extraordinary* increases quality by providing a child input with rarer vocabulary and better clarity of meaning. High-quality input will also combine more ideas together and embed one idea within another. Compare the quality in the following two examples:

1. His shirt was red. It was as red hot as fire. His shirt caught the sunlight.
2. The red of his shirt, as red hot as fire, caught the sunlight.

High-quality input may provide unique, creative, figurative, or poetic ways of stating an idea. For example, "His heart soared" may be seen as higher-quality input than "He was very excited."

Apply Your Knowledge: The following features of teachers' English language (#1–4) and adult language-building experience (#5) are indicators of the quality of classroom language input. Please rate yourself on the following characteristics of your English. (Rate yourself from 1 to 5, with 5 being the highest and 1 being the lowest.)

1.	English vocabulary size	1	2	3	4	5
2.	English pronunciation	1	2	3	4	5
3.	English talkativeness	1	2	3	4	5
4.	Correct sentence formation	1	2	3	4	5
5.	Amount of English reading	1	2	3	4	5

What thoughts do you have about performing this self-assessment?

There is an important set of reins preventing the quality horse from running too fast and too far away from EBs' grasp. When vocabulary is very challenging, the structure of sentences has a great deal of embedding and/or sentences are lengthy, or the language is very figurative and nonliteral, the difficulty of the language grows. High-quality language that can just be grasped with stretching and reaching, whether it is presented in text or orally, is very beneficial to language development. However, if there is too much stretching and reaching, children will be at risk of tumbling into incomprehension. Teachers need to be able to perform a quick-footed and skillful dance between providing challenging input and ensuring that children can understand the input.

Teaching Practice 1: Provide high-quality input during instruction and all other periods of the school day. Talk a lot and use rich vocabulary, challenging language structure, and sophisticated concepts.

Intake

Children must take into their minds and remember the input that is provided to them in order for their language to grow. Extensive and high-quality input that is not internalized will not lead to English growth. Imagine EB Houa, who is in a classroom in which the teacher reads informational books and storybooks twice a day. During book-reading time, Houa's attention is often captured by the activity occurring in a grassy area visible from where she sits. Houa is not likely to experience the possible English language development (ELD) growth afforded by the storybook input because she is not "intaking" the input. The most common impediments to language intake are shown in Figure 3.2.

Instructional practices and learning activities that respond to the challenges identified in Figure 3.2 will help children "take in" language input to their minds. A goal of ELD lessons should be to ensure that children want to participate. Lessons that are based on children's interests and that engage and support them emotionally will support language intake. This practice will also capitalize on the Wellsprings of Promise discussed in Chapter 1. To be sure, all material that is identified within PreK learning standards and K–2 content standards may not initially interest children. A highly skilled teacher will include in lessons practices to make even remote disciplinary content interesting and provide children with warm emotional support. The teacher who introduces children to the American Revolution by having a discussion on what rules in the school or classroom children find unfair or who asks children to examine new "proposed" classroom rules, some of which are unreasonable, can get children interested and started on understanding the reasons for the American Revolution. The teacher who smiles, marvels at children's contributions, and treats all responses as meaningful, even when correction is needed, provides a warm and supportive emotional climate. This climate is something children feel, and its presence encourages their oral language intake (and language output).

Figure 3.2. Challenges to Language Intake

- Child is not interested.
- Child is emotionally detached.
- Child is not attentive.
- Input is not effectively offered.
- Child does not understand the input.

When lessons are well planned, prepared, and enacted, children can attend better to the language input they are expected to learn. When pictures to show the new words are misplaced or the procedure to get into groups to talk about the new vocabulary is not clear, children's ability to intake language input is challenged. Perhaps it goes without saying, but bear with me: If children cannot understand the input, they will surely not intake it in a manner that connects the language with meaning. In classrooms all over America, children can recite the Pledge of Allegiance by heart and still have no idea of the meaning behind what they are saying. Adding nonverbal supports to instruction is a general principle for potentially increasing children's ability to understand language, a precondition for meaningful intake. Demonstrations, pictures, graphs, realia kits of miniature objects related to the language, demonstrations, and gestures are examples of nonverbal supports for acquiring language meaning. Providing explanations of new words and concepts, breaking language into smaller chunks, and a slight slowing of verbal delivery are verbal practices that can be helpful. These ideas are summarized in Figure 3.3.

Teaching Practice 2: Include in each lesson a plan for creating interest and emotional engagement.

Teaching Practice 3: Respond regularly and with warmth to all children's language.

Teaching Practice 4: Monitor each child's attention during language learning opportunities and employ emotionally positive practices for focusing children's attention on language.

Output

It is handy that the same features of input that lead to language intake are also important in language output. Recall that these features are amount and quality. The degree to which language production, or output, contributes to language acquisition has been one of the most hotly debated questions in the field of second language acquisition (SLA). There is increasing evidence that when children speak more and speak with language that is more sophisticated, they have higher levels of English proficiency (Swain, 2005). The reasons that language output, or speaking, leads to language learning are summarized in Figure 3.4.

Conversations between teachers and students that have more words are associated with greater English acquisition at the end of 1st grade (Aukrust & Rydland,

Figure 3.3. How Do I Increase Intake?

- Create language use situations where children want to participate and there is a warm emotional climate (interest, emotional engagement).
- Ensure that children are attending by fostering motivation and good management strategies (attention).
- Talk about things children have experience with (interest, attention, understanding).
- Let children lead and follow their lead during discussions while keeping the talk on point (interest, attention, understanding).
- Use language supported with demonstration, concrete realia, and gestures (understanding).
- Explain new words and concepts (understanding).
- Speak with slightly slower verbal delivery (understanding).

Apply Your Knowledge: On the lesson plan for the next ELD lesson you are going to teach, write the following questions in two to three places:

» Who is/was intaking the input and how do I know?
» How can I modify what I am doing to increase intake?

Answer these questions as you come to them in the lesson plan.

2011). A provocative recent finding is that the level of English proficiency of peers is also related to acquiring English for both PreK and kindergarten children (Gamez, 2015; Palermo et al., 2014). These studies mean that it is important for EBs to have peer interaction with more proficient speakers of English. It may seem appealing to place kids of similar levels of English together for ELD instruction. You may feel that this practice creates a comfortable setting for participation, and it solves the problem of differentiating English language level that is so troubling to teachers in mixed-proficiency groups. However, grouping children of varying levels together is more beneficial to their achievement. Why do you think this is so?

Greater attention to the benefit of output for language learning represents a change from earlier educational approaches to SLA. Earlier educational approaches for English language development emphasized input, particularly input that was *comprehensible* (understandable) to EBs, so fiercely that programs downplayed and, in some cases, forbade practices to elicit output. Current evidence has shown that these models were based on a misunderstanding of language development and produced children whose could understand language much better than they could speak. Therefore, language arts instruction that calls for and motivates the linguistic participation of EBs from the beginning of SLA is recommended.

There are three general learning conditions that can encourage language production even among the young, beginning, or reticent second language learners. The first condition is to provide lessons and learning activities that create a desire

Figure 3.4. How Does Language Output Consolidate Language Learning?

- Output makes language more concrete through information from the speech apparatus and body.
- Output is necessary to effectively use language with others.
- Output enhances language fluency and increases speed and ease in using language.
- Output provides self-feedback because children can "hear themselves talk."
- Output tests if language is understandable to others.
- Output helps language models provide input at the correct level of difficulty.
- Output allows peers to scaffold language level for one another.

to speak and, in fact, make it almost impossible not to speak. I like to think of the instructional challenge in terms of releasing children's oral production via effective instructional routines. I have observed children's absolute delight and need to speak when teachers make purposeful mistakes such as saying, "Here is a dog," when showing a picture of a cat. Interaction with peers around a topic of shared interest is also a compelling motivation for language production. One of my favorite effective practices to help release language production is the use of mouth and ear picture cards. Child can talk in pairs, taking turns to switch the ear (listening) card and mouth (talking) card (see Figure 3.5). The cards help make sure that everyone talks and everyone listens.

A second condition for encouraging language production is to provide emotionally safe production opportunities. Figure 3.6 lists a number of practices that encourage and elicit language output or production.

A third condition for eliciting language production is to structure production requests that are sensitive to the child's level of language skill. Novices can be given questions that can be answered with a simple "yes" or "no." Children with a little more proficiency can be provided with partial sentences to complete. Those with the highest levels of proficiency can be asked questions that elicit a full utterance. Examples of different levels of questions beginning with those for children with lowest levels of proficiency that might be used for discussing the story *Little Red Riding Hood* follow:

- Was the Big Bad Wolf a good animal? (yes, no)
- Did the Big Bad Wolf like Little Red Riding Hood? (yes, no)
- The Big Bad Wolf wanted to ________. (partial sentence to complete)
- Tell two things about the Big Bad Wolf.

Teachers report that creating different levels of prompts according to children's English proficiency is difficult. It will be very helpful initially to explicitly write out prompts in lesson plans for children of different proficiency levels. With consistent (daily) practice, you will find yourself becoming adept at differentiating prompts to elicit language. You will see your growing skill in the frequency and ease with which children respond.

Figure 3.5. Listening and Talking Cards

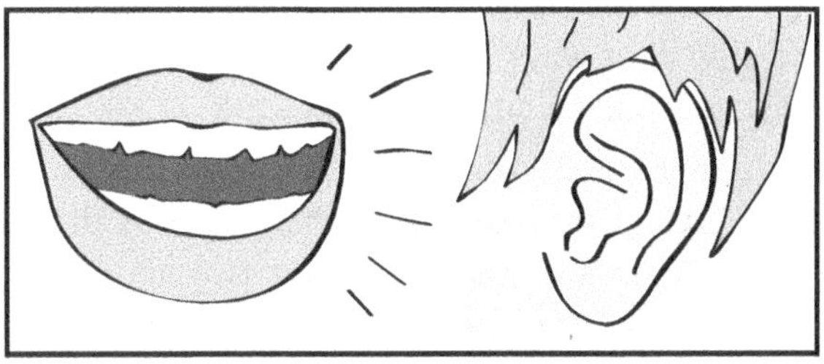

Figure 3.6. Emotionally Safe Language Elicitation Practices

- Group recitation of repeated poems and nursery rhymes
- Choral (group) responding and singing
- Peer partner "talk to your buddy" activities
- Use of puppets, props, and other concrete supports
- Participation in conversations about well-known books
- Repeated singing of songs
- Rereading books and having children chime in
- Retelling familiar books
- Individual pretend reading of familiar and new books
- Chanting along with predictable books and repeated book reading
- Instructions and routines with repeated and predictable structures
- Use of gesture and pointing to illustrations to help children access meaning
- Questions and prompts scaffolded to the child's level of English proficiency

Teaching Practice 5: Group children with more proficient speakers of English.

Teaching Practice 6: Ensure that children talk a great deal using rich vocabulary and challenging language structures.

Teaching Practice 7: Provide emotionally safe conditions when eliciting language production (speaking).

Teaching Practice 8: Use prompts aligned with the child's level of English proficiency to elicit language.

Balancing Instruction in Language Form and Language Meaning

Traditionally, ELD instruction for young EBs emphasized language meaning over language form. *Language form* refers to how pieces of language are put together according to the rules of a particular language. For example, English speakers are expected to say "the green tree," while speakers of French would say the equivalent

> *Apply Your Knowledge:* Select a child from your class who uses little English in the classroom. Using the chart on Emotionally Safe Language Elicitation Practices as a guide, plan three ways you could entice this child into English language usage. Try them out and modify them as needed.

of "the tree green." Chinese speakers may "legally" say the equivalent of "two hat" while speakers of English are expected to say "two hats."

It seems logical that because communication of meaning is the purpose of language, it should be the focus of instruction. Indeed, practices to help children understand and express meaning is essential. Yet, command of the structures of the language is also necessary to support children's ability to understand and express meaning. Three subsystems of language called *phonology* (the rules related to individual sounds used to construct words), *syntax* (rules for how words can be combined together), *morphology* (rules for how individual words are structured to reflect changes in meaning such as making plurals or representing past tense) are typically considered the main categories of language form. Figure 3.7 shows examples of these three subsystems. A recent study found that only 6% of the time allocated for ELD was spent in teaching language form or structure (Saunders, Foorman, & Carlson, 2006). EBs need planned and explicit daily instruction in language meaning and language form. Form and meaning waltz together gracefully in perfect step in language competence.

Teaching Practice 9: Provide daily instruction in language form/structure and language meaning .

Recall that the amount and quality of the language input children hear is a powerful contributor to English oral proficiency. Teachers are typically the individuals within the classroom who have the strongest English language competencies, and children typically hear more language from teachers than from anyone else in the classroom. Therefore, the quality of the language input from the teacher has a strong influence on children's ultimate level of English proficiency. And yet, there is evidence that

> *Apply Your Knowledge:* What are three things you could do to continue developing your personal oral language? Here are some ideas to help you get started: Join a book club, play online vocabulary building games, subscribe to magazines on topics you are interested in, take a creative writing course in adult education, or join a drama group.
>
> List two ideas for professional development topics that would help you strengthen your personal oral language. Think outside the box!

Figure 3.7. Examples of Three Language Subsystems

Language subsystem	Example 1	Example 2
Phonology	Children tap out the number of sounds in the word "cat."	Children use mirrors to watch their mouth while they practice saying alphabet letter sounds.
Syntax/ Morphology	Children correct teacher errors: "She no eat the apple."	Children combine two sentences: "He got the milk." "He poured the milk."
	"The dog runned away."	Children use play animals and have them do different actions while saying what that action is: "The dog is running," The horse is jumping," and so on.

many PreK–2 teachers' personal knowledge and sophisticated use of phonology, syntax, and morphology may need bolstering (Dickinson, 2011). For this reason, in Chapter 4 I will elaborate how to teach ELD in a manner that enacts the waltz of language meaning and language structure.

The Importance of Teacher-Child Interaction in Language Development

Conversations or more extended interactions are particularly good at facilitating language learning for both EF and EB young children. When Ms. Garcia and Lucas take turns going back and forth discussing what each of them did over the weekend, the stage is set for language growth. When the proper research-based language and relationship conditions are added in, children are mesmerized, inspired, and eager to "language along," stretching their existing abilities to new levels because they are so linguistically and emotionally engaged. The language (input, intake, and output) and relationship conditions leading to language growth can be represented and remembered with the acronym *ERECT Language*. Figure 3.8 shows the language practices represented by each letter in the ERECT Language model.

Ms. Chertia sits at the table with Irina, makes eye contact, and smiles. This simple act signals to Irina that Ms. Chertia is opening the door to interaction. Irina's response to this overture will almost certainly be eagerness for what comes next. Eye contact and emotional engagement has been initiated. Ms. Chertia asks Irina what she is drawing, and Irina replies, "I am making swing." Ms. Chertia then asks, "Did you go on a swing?" If the child is more proficient, the teacher might ask, "Did you go on a swing and pump your legs to go higher and higher?" accompanied by leg movements and a hand swinging to illustrate the words *pumping* and *higher*. This question shows enactment of the ERECT idea of "Responding to what children

Figure 3.8. ERECT Language

E is for Eye contact and emotional engagement.
R is for Responding to what children say.
E is for Expanding and elaborating on what children say.
C is for Clarifying what children say with questions and rephrasing.
T is for Taking turns and sharing the talking space.

say." Responsiveness establishes the positive emotional and relationship conditions for language growth. Expanding and elaborating on what children say and encouraging them to do the same is a mechanism for language growth. Expanding and elaborating teacher responses from Ms. Chertia might be "Are there other things from a playground in your picture?" or "I see some other things in your picture (point). What are they?" Ms. Chertia might ask, "Where did you go to swing?" or "Who are all of the people I see in your picture?" to clarify what Irina is drawing. Finally, it is important for teachers and children to share the talking space. When teachers talk more and children talk more, when they take turns, English growth can be higher than when teachers dominate the language production space.

Teachers of course, are constrained in their ability to engage in conversations and extended interactions because of the number of children in classrooms and the length of the school day. The more that a teacher is able to achieve this ideal, the more support for ELD she or he is providing. My hope is that drawing attention to the significance of these interactions for ELD and elaborating on how to enact these interactions with the ERECT model will encourage you to capture more minutes for conversation and extended interactions during informal parts of the day, small-group activities, independent seat work for older children, or even large-group instruction.

Teaching Practice 10: Expand the frequency of teacher-child conversations and extended interactions.

Teaching Practice 11: Use the principles of ERECTing Language while talking with children.

UNDERSTANDING ENGLISH-PROFICIENCY DEVELOPMENT

How Much Does Play Contribute to Language Development?

There have been strong claims over many years for the value of play in language development. A more nuanced and careful view of the research shows that it is play of a certain kind that supports language development (Mages, 2008). Think about the following play scenarios: (1) Annabelle playing with blocks alone in the science

Apply Your Knowledge: Use the following set of questions to reflect upon how much you use the ERECT model. Rate yourself from 1 to 5, with 5 being the highest and 1 being the lowest. Where are your strengths? Where are you less strong? How can you grow?
ERECTing Language

1. Make Eye contact and emotional connection when talking with children?
   1 2 3 4 5
2. Respond to children's oral language overtures to you:
   Individually?
   1 2 3 4 5
   In small groups?
   1 2 3 4 5
   In large groups?
   1 2 3 4 5
3. Expand and elaborate what children say with interesting ideas, more complex language, and new words?
   1 2 3 4 5
4. Clarify what children are trying to say (through questions)?
   1 2 3 4 5
5. Take turns in talking with children?
   1 2 3 4 5

center; (2) Caroline cooking a meal in the playhouse, while Vang plays with the baby alongside her; (3) a small group of children building blocks to form a city in a jungle, while a family is out gathering food; (4) the same scenario as 3 but a teacher, books and a video clip about the jungle are added. The teacher helps children change roles from being a queen at one time to becoming a monkey a little later. She asks questions such as "Who are the residents of the city?" and "How will the family get food for their dinner?" There are science books and a video clip on the computer about jungles that children can explore as they play. Which scenario is most likely to lead to language growth? You probably picked the last one, and you would be correct. But exactly what are the features of play that make this last scenario with a teacher present more likely to promote language?

The play in the final scenario above involves imagination and pretend. The jungle theme helps children learn to make a connected story. Creating stories is a language ability associated with comprehension of oral and written language. There is an adult present, who is not too obtrusive but is stimulating language. The books and video build children's conceptual and linguistic knowledge about jungles. When children change roles, they use more varied language and learn to adjust their language based on the role they are playing. The collaborative group engages children and helps them use extended chunks of language.

You are almost certainly aware of the difficulties in finding time or establishing the academic value of play in contemporary education. I believe there are opportunities to implement some of the properties of play that support language development while achieving PreK standards, CCSS, and state standards, particularly for social studies content. Pause here and think for a moment: "How might I create a theme-based activity related to social studies learning objectives, supported with social studies language, materials and questions related to the social studies objectives? How could children collaborate, change roles, and create extended strands of imaginary and pretend play accompanied by language? The themes of community and family, transportation, the city, and the like are ones that come to mind as having potential for developing justifiable play-like activities that capitalize on some of the features of play that support language. One idea is to have children learn about and then play several of the roles of different members of a community. What do you think?

Teaching Practice 12: Use collaborative groups with pretend and imaginary play-like scenarios where children take on various roles and create theme-related extended dialogues accompanied by language-building materials and teacher language stimulation.

Is There a Silent Stage in Second Language Acquisition?

Many PreK–2 teachers have been taught that children typically experience a period of silence, or nonverbalness, early in second language acquisition. In addition, children are portrayed as being engaged in active language learning even if they may not be producing language. Some believe teachers should not expect or press for language use until children begin to use language on their own and that there may even be negative emotional and SLA consequences for expecting children to use English before they begin to use it on their own. I recently conducted a reexamination of all of the evidence I could find related to the claim that silence is typical of and beneficial to second language learning. This examination led to the strong conclusion that (1) there is very little basis for the presence of a silent period in SLA, and (2) there is almost no evidence that it is beneficial to SLA (Roberts, 2014).

Earlier in this chapter, the positive contributions to language development afforded by talking were explained and practices to elicit talking were presented. The value of output and the lack of support for the existence of a silent stage in SLA is the foundation for the recommendation that ELD instruction should include expectations and opportunities for English oral production from the beginning of second language learning.

Teaching Practice 13: Expect, elicit, and support oral language production (speaking) from the beginning of second language acquisition.

Apply Your Knowledge: Review the content or themes that you teach in social studies. Select one that lends itself to the type of play-like interaction described above. Plan one collaborative activity related to the theme where children can cooperatively take on imaginary and pretend roles. What materials, such as vocabulary cards, topic-related books, and videos, could be integrated there? What would be your role to spark language during this collaborative activity?

Should English Language Development Instruction Be Provided During an ELD Block or Integrated Throughout the Day?

Educators often discuss whether ELD instruction should occur in a separate block of time or if it should be integrated throughout the day. Two studies of kindergarten programs found higher levels of English proficiency growth when ELD instruction was provided in a block rather than distributed throughout the day (Gamez, 2015; Saunders, Foorman, & Carlson, 2006). The question of the effectiveness of blocked or integrated ELD instruction within preschool classrooms has not been answered. Answering this question is important because preschool philosophy and standards are based on the assumption that English language development will proceed best when it is integrated within meaningful and thematic activities throughout the day. Increasing emphasis on teaching language structure across the PreK–2 span is likely to make blocked ELD even more beneficial.

Teaching Practice 14: Provide specific English language development instruction in a block.

DISTINGUISHING BETWEEN COMMUNICATIVE AND ACADEMIC ENGLISH PROFICIENCY

Educational Principle 2: Develop ELD programs for both communicative and academic language.

Communicative proficiency refers to the ability to use language to manage your day. It is the everyday talk used to communicate with others and to accomplish activities and routines both in and out of classrooms. When children tell one another what they want, explain disputes to an adult, figure out where they can get a new box of crayons, or share personal experiences and interests, they are using communicative language. This form of language is urgently important, particularly to the youngest beginners learning English. It overlaps with but can be distinguished from academic language.

Academic language differs from functional, everyday talk in that it conforms more to formal grammar rules. Content-area language within science, math, and social studies is academic. Content-area language has unique language structure features and vocabulary. It is also more likely to expose children to concepts, places, times, and things they have not experienced—that is, it is decontextualized from ongoing activity or supportive context. For example, decontextualized language would be used to describe an imaginary land or to learn about Native American history from informational text. Facility with decontextualized language is particularly important in reading (Genesee, Lindholm-Leary, Saunders, & Christian, 2006).

The use of decontextualized language advances children's language, learning, and thinking by increasing their capacity to rely on language by itself as a tool for learning. This ability to learn from and think with language by itself, devoid of prior or ongoing concrete experiences, is at the heart of academic achievement. To learn about Alaskan Inuit society or the physical properties of light will require children to learn with decontextualized language. Experience with decontextualized language is an especially significant challenge for at-risk children. Children's competence in using this type of language can be developed orally in preschool and kindergarten and with text as children's reading skill increases.

Teaching Practice 15: Provide opportunities to use decontextualized English by talking about past and future events, imaginary worlds, and content-area topics (math, science, social studies).

Both communicative and academic English development should be included in ELD programs. Development of EBs' ability to learn from decontextualized first language will provide a linguistic foundation for L2 language and literacy achievement. Helping families increase their use of decontextualized L1 should be a priority.

You can suggest that they engage in the following oral language practices:

- Talk about things from the past and the future.
- Use language during pretend play.
- Expose children to storybooks and informational texts that introduce them to new experiences.
- Use language to create imaginary and pretend experiences.

In addition, Figure 3.9 provides overall guidance for how families can help strengthen their EB children's English proficiency.

Teaching Practice 16: Provide families with specific ideas for using decontextualized first language.

> *Apply Your Knowledge:* Take a favorite read-aloud book. Go through it and write three questions that would encourage children to respond with academic/decontextualized language. Identify 5–10 vocabulary words that you could teach and then use to talk about things "not in the present" with children.

THE PREK-GRADE 2 CONTINUUM: STRENGTHENING ENGLISH PROFICIENCY

The same basic processes of receiving input, taking in the input, and producing output characterize ELD from PreK through grade 2. A teacher who is warmly responsive to children's language and uses children's language as a guide for his or her own subsequent responses will add to children's English competence. Thinking about ELD across the PreK–2 time span highlights the importance of both communicative competence and academic language competence.

The increasing emphasis on academic language and disciplinary learning (science, social studies, history) from PreK through grade 2 means that teachers will need to develop sophisticated skill in responding with warmth to children's talk while at the same time achieving the lesson goals and teaching the designated content. Remembering that language learning requires not only teacher input within a lesson, but also child intake and output, will help achieve the needed instructional balance. Imagine a lesson on water conservation that includes information on the purposes of dams and reservoirs. LaMelle enthusiastically states that "Gutters are dams." A skillful teacher might ask, "LaMelle, how is a gutter like a dam?" This gives LaMelle the opportunity to respond, "The stuff and leaves in the gutter make a dam for the water when it rains." The teacher responds, "I see—the leaves hold back a small amount of water like a dam. Dams for water conservation are much bigger and are built from something very strong and that will last a long time like concrete—it is a permanent dam." Notice that this skilled teacher responds positively to LaMelle's comment and develops it to help teach the class about the goal and content of the lesson.

In preschool classrooms, communicative language may be emphasized more than academic language. Reasons for the emphasis on everyday talk include the fact that PreK EBs are typically all novice learners of English, there is a strong emphasis on social–emotional development, and everyday talk may support social–emotional development by focusing on language that helps children share toys, find a play partner, or talk with others during family-style meals. At PreK, the conditions for eliciting output may need particular focus because many PreK EBs are at the very beginning of English acquisition. In comparison, language in K–2 classrooms will increasingly draw on the use of academic/decontextualized language as the curriculum becomes increasingly academic. The importance of developing competence in everyday talk may fall to the wayside.

Figure 3.9. How to Engage Families in Strengthening Their Emergent Bilingual Children's English Proficiency

- Create a regular at-home program in which children are assigned to teach specific elements of English (vocabulary, language structure) that they are learning to family member (adults, younger and older siblings).
- Help families understand that developing the first language will help English acquisition.
- Provide English labels for common items in the home, including those that are already labeled in the first language.
- Help families expand children's experiences and world knowledge through outings, exploration, and talking about all of these things.
- Help families understand why and how to provide for daily quiet time for children to pretend read, read, and write about things they choose.
- Help families locate and gain access to libraries and other community sources of children's books and educational digital media (library cards, registrations, websites, and so on).
- Provide families information on free or low-cost resources for children in their community.
- Make specific suggestions for home and community experiences to expand background knowledge related to classroom units of study.
- Make recommendations for specific English TV channels, programs, websites, and apps to support language and literacy learning.

CONNECTIONS TO THE COMMON CORE STATE STANDARDS AND PRESCHOOL LEARNING STANDARDS

The CCSS have a strong emphasis on the input and output components of English language development. This emphasis is largely found within the listening and speaking standards. A noteworthy aspect of these standards is the companion emphasis on collaborative talk among students. Collaboration has the potential to be very beneficial for EBs. The properties of effective collaboration are expanded upon in Chapter 4. The emphasis on children's competence with language structure within the CCSS is a particularly welcome one that will require significant support and professional development (PD) for teachers because it has not received much previous emphasis.

Preschool standards focus on children's growth in expressive and receptive language aligned with the research on the typical course of language acquisition. This approach is appropriate because the course of first and second language English development is highly similar. Most of the standards focus on communicative and social language use rather than academics or decontextualized language use. Thus the more social standards for PreK and more academic-oriented standards for K–2 are consistent with major goals and purposes of the two types of programs

Educational Principles from Chapter 3

1. Include teacher personal language development as a centerpiece and valid component of professional development.
2. Develop ELD programs for both communicative and academic language.

Teaching Practices from Chapter 3

1. Provide high-quality input during instruction and all other periods of the school day. Talk a lot and use rich vocabulary, challenging language structure, and sophisticated concepts.
2. Include in each lesson a plan for creating interest and emotional engagement.
3. Respond regularly and with warmth to all children's language.
4. Monitor each child's attention during language learning opportunities and employ emotionally positive practices for focusing attention on language.
5. Group children with more proficient speakers of English.
6. Ensure that children talk a lot using rich vocabulary and challenging language structures.
7. Provide emotionally safe conditions when eliciting language production (speaking).
8. Use prompts aligned with the child's level of English proficiency to elicit language.
9. Provide daily instruction in language meaning and language form/structure.
10. Expand the frequency of teacher-child conversations and extended interactions.
11. Use the principles of ERECTing Language while talking with children.
12. Use collaborative groups with pretend and imaginary play-like scenarios where children take on various roles and create theme-related extended dialogues accompanied by language-building materials and teacher language stimulation.
13. Expect, elicit, and support oral language production (speaking) from the beginning of second language acquisition.
14. Provide specific English language development instruction in a block.
15. Provide opportunities to use decontextualized English by talking about past and future events, imaginary worlds, and content-area topics (math, science, social studies).
16. Provide families with specific ideas for using decontextualized first language.

CHAPTER 4

Teaching Language Structure

IMPORTANT RESEARCH FINDINGS ABOUT LANGUAGE STRUCTURE

- » Integrating instruction on language structure with language activities focusing on meaning is the most effective way to teach language structure.
- » Knowledge and skillful use of language structure supports EBs' oral language development and literacy learning.
- » Language output is particularly beneficial for acquiring knowledge and skill related to English language structure.
- » Collaboration with peers in mixed-proficiency groups is beneficial for learning language structure.
- » The organization and learning activities within collaborative groups affect how much English language is learned.
- » Teachers' knowledge of language structure and its relationship to early literacy instruction needs bolstering.

Emergent bilinguals' knowledge of and skill in using language structure, or language form, is one of several language competencies upon which reading and writing achievement is dependent. A fitting definition, taken from the Merriam-Webster online dictionary, defines *structure* as "something arranged in a definite pattern of organization." Within this chapter, the terms *form* and *structure* are used interchangeably.

In this chapter, the major components of language form to include in instruction will be explained and instructional practices to teach them identified. I will review briefly the history of the heated debates regarding the amount and methodology of instruction that best helps EBs learn second language form. Recommendations for new approaches to ELD based on current research will be explained and related teaching practices identified.

The main idea to be developed is that language form should be taught with explicit lessons during real communication. The kind of talk that is most effective is orderly and typically involves staying on point with an idea over the course of several sentences. This kind of talk is called *discourse*. Discourse is longer than a phrase or sentence. Discourse occurs within oral discussion, storybooks, informational texts, and writing. Children should learn how to speak all of the English sounds; how to order the words put together to talk about ideas, things, and actions; and a myriad of other aspects of language structure while they are responding to oral and written discourse (text) and constructing meaningful discourse about academic and personal experience.

Teaching language form while children talk about topics and experiences that are meaningful to them is called *form-focused meaning instruction.* This type of instruction is consistent with the latest research. It dovetails with the emphasis on students' competence to think in complex ways with sophisticated language about large chunks of oral or written language within CCSS and PreK standards. The special topics of correcting children's language form errors and the value of correct English pronunciation are considered.

This chapter will also address the critical role of appropriate collaboration and talk among children from PreK through grade 2 and how to provide it. I will identify the challenges for teaching language structure to EBs and suggest necessary "beyond-the-classroom" supports needed by many teachers.

I hope you come away from this chapter with a sense of conviction and urgency about the importance of teaching language structure to EBs and that you have a clearer picture of what domains of language structure to teach with this picture framed by what is included in the CCSS and PreK standards. I also hope you feel better prepared to teach language structure and are inspired enough to try some of the practices identified in the chapter even before you finish reading it.

THE FOUR DOMAINS OF ENGLISH LANGUAGE STRUCTURE

Educational Principle 1: Develop instructional programs that include explicit and regular goals for teaching EBs the structure of the English language (phonology, morphology, syntax, and semantics).

During instruction, teachers explain, define, model, illustrate, practice, and provide children with feedback on many aspects of language structure. These lessons include concepts about the four domains of English language form:

1. Phonology—the individual linguistic sounds, called phonemes, that are combined to form different words
2. Morphology—units of meaning, or morphemes, including root words and modifications of them, such as pluralization
3. Syntax and grammar—rules on how phrases and sentences are correctly constructed that tell you to say the "the green tree" (in English) rather than "the tree green"
4. Semantics—the meaning of words, phrases, sentences, and discourses

The language structure EBs have learned in their first language acts as a filter through which they process English. The filter is a porous one, but it will influence the process of learning the rules and structures that govern English. For example, when children whose first language is Chinese say "two shoe" instead of "two shoes" in English, they are showing a first language influence based on Chinese morphology that does not use a "marker" for plural words. PreK–2 children will learn the rules that govern English phonology, morphology, syntax and semantics as they acquire English. Explicit instruction can improve their accuracy and help quicken their pace.

Teaching Practice 1: Provide daily instruction in the sound structure (phonology), word structure (morphology), sentence structure (syntax), and semantic structure (vocabulary and discourse) of English.

> *Apply Your Knowledge:* List 8-12 errors in English language structure that you frequently observe among EBs in your classroom. Write the four headings phonology, morphology, syntax, and semantics on a piece of paper and categorize each error into the correct column. What can you learn from this list? What does it suggest to you about teaching EBs in your classroom? If you have difficulty identifying 8-12 errors, spend some time listening to your EBs talk to discover them.

Phonology

There are 44 phonemes in the English phoneme inventory. Other languages have between 15 and more than 100 phonemes. Each phoneme is created by a specific configuration of the speech apparatus that includes the tongue, lips, teeth, throat, palate, and how air moves through them. Producing sounds in oral language is called *articulation*. Phonemes are arranged into different sequences to create different spoken words. For example, changing the phoneme /h/ in the word *hat* to the phoneme /b/ changes the meaning from something you wear on your head to something that you hit a ball with. Changing one phoneme creates a totally new meaning. It may occur to you that this total number of phonemes is different from the 26 letters of the alphabet. Therein lies one of the challenges for learning to read and write in English (see Chapter 5 for elaboration).

It is important for children to have in their heads a clear and accurate idea of each phoneme and the ability to say it accurately. If children's English speech phonemes are fuzzy, indistinct, or incomplete, the clarity of their speech production and speech perception is likely to be affected. Their progress in learning letter names, sounds, print patterns, and decoding may also be hampered (Elbro, 1996; Roberts, 2005). This is because learning to read and write well relies on the ability to accurately and quickly connect elements of speech (phonemes) and print.

Instruction in English phonology can speed EBs along in learning the English phoneme inventory. This instruction will help them distinguish English phonemes and articulate them correctly in spoken language. Research has demonstrated the benefits of this type of instruction for the clarity of speech and reading acquisition (Boyer & Ehri, 2011). If you are uncertain about the accuracy of your phoneme articulation, you can consult certain apps and the Internet for instruction. In one of my research projects, families asked for help with saying (articulating) English letter sounds correctly. We made CDs and sent them home for families to use.

Teaching Practice 2: Teach children how to correctly produce English phonemes.

Morphology

The English domain of morphology includes rules about individual words that govern how they may be modified to change meanings. Each word is a morpheme with rules governing how to change meaning, such as by adding (/s/, /z/) to indicate more than one, appending endings to words to refer to the present or past (jumping, jumped), and to construct comparatives (big, bigger, biggest).

Teaching Practice 3: Teach children the morphology rules for how to modify word structure to indicate past and present tense, comparatives, plurals, meanings associated with prefixes and suffixes, and other aspects of morphology consistent with their level of English language proficiency.

Syntax

The English domain of syntax refers to the rules that govern how words are put together in phrases and sentences. Changes in syntax can affect meaning. "Kean fell on the car" means something very different from "The car fell on Kean." Syntax is often thought of as "grammar." The CCSS category *Conventions of Standard English* corresponds loosely to syntax and morphology, as presented later in this chapter.

Teaching Practice 4: Teach children syntactic rules for how to structure simple sentences and how to combine and embed sentences.

Semantics

The English domain of semantics refers to the meaning part of language. It includes knowledge at the word, phrase, sentence, and discourse levels. Semantic advancement is the ultimate goal of oral language and literacy. Achievement of that advancement is dependent upon phonological, morphological, and syntactic advancement. Semantics does not stand alone. Vocabulary knowledge is part of semantics and is such an important area for advancing EBs' oral and written proficiency that I devote

Chapter 6 to this topic. Reading comprehension, oral presentation, collaborative group interaction, and all areas of listening, speaking, reading, and writing have semantic communication as their goal.

Apply Your Knowledge: Make four columns on a sheet of paper. Label them phonology, morphology, syntax, and semantics. Take the ELD curriculum used in your class or the language structure lessons that you have taught and categorize activities into the four domains.

If this is manageable for you, you are on your way to knowing how to provide comprehensive ELD instruction. If this is difficult for you, study the information about the domains of language in this chapter. To find additional explanations, consult the Internet with the search terms teaching phonology in ESL, teaching morphology in ESL, teaching syntax in ESL, and teaching semantics in ESL.

FORM-FOCUSED-MEANING INSTRUCTION

Many teachers believe that because they model and teach language all day, children will implicitly learn sufficient language structure. Indeed, when teacher language exemplifies correct structure, English proficiency can grow. The accuracy of this belief has been at the center of the debate on how to best make sure that EB children learn language structure.

Reviewing Past Views

There has been a history of contention and inconsistency about how best to help EBs acquire English language structure in classroom settings. For our purposes, the most important area of contention has been which teaching methodologies may be beneficial and to what degree. Recall the concept of *input* discussed in Chapter 3. Related is *comprehensible input,* which incorporates a very strong belief that children acquire increasing levels of knowledge of language structure informally—implicitly—from the input. Under this view, all children possess an inborn mental Language Acquisition Device (LAD). In the presence of language input, this language-voracious LAD would be unleashed to acquire language and particularly language structure. Scientists call this a Nativist perspective.

The importance of *comprehensible input* was a refinement of the Nativist perspective. The teacher's primary role for language acquisition was to provide a flood of comprehensible language input. According to the concept of comprehensible input, the LAD was assumed to be in its highest gear when second language input challenged children at the upper limit of their ability to comprehend. This refined Nativist view led to practices derived from the belief that EBs' lack of L2 usage was expected, accepted, and even potentially beneficial to second language attainment (Roberts, 2014). Instruction on language form was viewed as unnecessary and potentially harmful. Recent critique has suggested that this belief contributed to a laissez-faire approach to providing language support services for EBs (August & Shanahan, 2008; Roberts, 2014). Instructional practice and ELD programs based on this belief continue to hold sway today, and many current teachers trained in ELD have this background.

Utilizing Effective Approaches to ELD

Current research evidence reveals that regular and explicit instruction targeting language structure is an important component of an excellent program to build EBs' English proficiency (Ellis, 2005). Research also reveals that embedding form-focused instruction within language exercises that are rich in meaning and mentally engage the learner is the most effective way to ensure that language structure is learned. This type of instruction is referred to as *form-focused meaning*. For example, a form-focused-meaning lesson on the past tense (a grade 1 Common Core standard) might include an oral discussion of what children had done over the weekend (PreK) or reading a text on the history of toys (grade 1–2). Past tense language forms will be needed in these discourses. If the lesson goal and activities focus only on extracting and expressing meaning, there will be less learning of the past tense language form. A tricky thing for both teacher and learner is not to let meaning take more than its fair share of the learning space when the goal is to teach language structure. State-of-the-art instruction to teach language structure will embody these new methods.

Teaching Practice 5: Limit the number of language forms to learn to one to two per lesson.

The major components you should include in each form-focused-meaning lesson are the following:

- Explain the target form.
- Provide multiple exposures to the target form.
- Engage students in meaningful language discourse.
- Include a method for drawing attention to the target form.
- Have activities that elicit the form, preferably collaborative ones.
- Include tasks to manage and manipulate the form.
- Include feedback and correction on children's use of the form.

An extended lesson example on regular and irregular plural nouns is provided in Figure 4.1. I suggest that you study the lesson, particularly if language form instruction is new to you. I hope you can learn from the lesson what these forms are, if you are not already sure of them!

Figure 4.1. Form-Focused Lesson Embedded Within Language Meaning: English Regular and Irregular Plural Nouns (Grade 2 Common Core Standard)

- Teacher introduces a picture of an aquarium filled with fish, rocks, and different types of plants.
- Children and teacher count together: 1 fish, 1 rock, and 1 plant.
- Teacher and children count together __ rocks and __ plants.
- Teacher: Hear the /s/ sound? You say /s/ when there is more than 1 thing.
- Children count the rocks and plants with a partner (1 rock, 2 rocks, 3 rocks, . . .)
- Teacher: You don't always say /s/ when there is more than 1 thing. Get ready. There are 1, 2 fish. I didn't say 2 fishes! Fish is an irregular plural. Say it with me.
- Different levels of practice items for children of different levels of English:
    - » Can you say 1 rock, 3 rocks? (easiest)
    - » There are_______, ______, and _____in the aquarium.
    - » What do you see in the aquarium? (hardest)
- *Teacher:* Tomorrow you will learn other words that have a special word for when there is more than 1. I have them on the language structure wall. (Teacher points to a picture of one tooth and 4 teeth; 1 man and 2 men; 1 foot and 3 feet.)
- *Teacher:* Try to find other irregular plural words for the lesson on language structure tomorrow.
- The next form lesson includes more practice with body parts that is part of the science curriculum.

Moving Beyond the Word, Phrase, and Sentence Level

Knowledge of language structure, or form, includes mastering extended hunks of language that are tied together through shared meaning. Yet, most ELD instruction on language structure occurs at the word, sentence, or phrase level. Practice of past tense verbs in individual and isolated sentences does not provide children with the naturalistic and communicative language experience that characterizes human language use. In addition, the combining of language form instruction within discourse can provide students with additional experience using academic language. A very important reason for including form-focused instruction within meaningful discourse is that it motivates children to talk and thereby acquire the multiple benefits that output can provide.

Teaching Practice 6: Teach language structure while children engage in extended, connected, and meaningful discourse.

Figure 4.2. How to Engage Families in Emergent Bilinguals' Learning of Language Structure

- Assign children regular at-home activities to explain to family members the features of English language structure they have just learned in class.
- Help families learn to expand upon what children say and to use longer sentences when they talk to children.

How Language Output Helps Children Learn Language Structure

The general input-intake-output process that leads to second language acquisition and the reasons why output is an important contributor to acquisition have been previously discussed in Chapter 3. Children talking together in student collaborations, during class discussions, in practice exercises during ELD, or in analytic activities related to texts or oral discourse all have the potential to play a special role in learning language structure. (See also Figure 4.2 for how to engage families in helping their children learn language structure.)

When children produce language that shares meaning (which can include communication about academic topics), they will receive feedback from others about the comprehensibility of their language. On many painful occasions, I have observed novice English learners in preschool and kindergarten classrooms attempting to express something in English and their speech not being understood. When children produce language, they receive concrete linguistic feedback by hearing and feeling the motor movements of their speech apparatus. To experience this yourself, take a paper towel roll and bend it into the shape of an L. Put the short end of the L to your mouth and the other to your ear. Say your name into the roll. Say the first phoneme of your name. What did you notice? You should have sensed that you could kind of hear yourself speak.

The Importance of Correction

Some teachers worry that correction may inhibit children's language production or lower self-confidence or self-esteem because of the very personal nature of language. However, correction can actually help EBs learn English structure when it occurs during lessons where children and teachers share a goal of learning language structure, when it is done with sensitivity and respect, when it does not unduly quash communication, and when it is focused on the learning goals that are within the language development zone for children to learn.

There are a number of different ways that correction can be made. Ranging on a continuum from least direct to most direct, these methods include modeling, clarifying, eliciting, and providing correct repetition. Correction that is direct and elicits a few correct repetitions is more effective than simply modeling. These differences are illustrated with a single example in Figure 4.3.

Figure 4.3. Continuum of Methods of Correction

Child Sentence	Teacher Response	Type of Correction
I no see the dog!	Oh, you don't see the dog?	Modeling
	Do you mean you don't see the dog?	Clarifying
	I'm sorry you can't find it. Can you say "I don't see the dog"?	Eliciting
	The same as above but add, Yes, can you say it one more time?	Eliciting with repetition

As a teacher, you may wonder if you should respond to the inevitable mispronunciations of individual words or phonemes within words that occur when children are learning a second language. Perhaps you know, as I do, educated adults who say *Valentimes Day* (instead of Valentine's Day), *supposebly* (supposedly), and *pacifically* (specifically). The question is: Does the quality of second language pronunciation matter? The straightforward answer is: Yes, accurate pronunciation matters. Speaking phonemes and words accurately increases communication and encourages further speaking because EBs receive affirmation that their language is effective. Accurate production of phonemes is also important for learning reading foundations. More information on pronunciation and reading is found in Chapter 5.

Teaching Practice 7: Favor correction that elicits the correct language form and repetition of it while maintaining a stance as a collaborative partner.

COLLABORATING WITH PEERS TO LEARN LANGUAGE FORM

Collaborative practices have the potential to draw upon EBs' unique linguistic, cultural, familial, and individual experiences of the world and to motivate meaningful English use. These learner strengths have been seriously overlooked in classroom instruction (August & Shanahan, 2008). Chapters 2, 3, and 8 include further explanation, teaching practices, and exercises to help you marshal these funds of knowledge. In addition, language production in group learning requires children to plan and execute into language what they want to say. This planning and executing requires phonological, morphological, syntactic, and semantic orchestration. Another important benefit of student collaboration is that children can and will adjust their language input for one another and thereby provide input that may be well matched to the speaker's oral English level. This potential of collaboration will be capitalized upon when children are taught what to do when misunderstanding occurs (see Figure 4.4).

In short, all of the potential benefits to language structure provided by output can be activated during collaboration. However, these benefits do not accrue automatically. The structure of the group and the activities need to be carefully planned.

Figure 4.4. Teaching Children What to Do when Language Is Not Understood

If a child doesn't understand what others children are saying, tell him or her:

» Say that you do not understand.
» Ask the child to repeat.
» Say what you think he or she means.
» Check if this correct.

If a child is not understood by other children, tell him or her:

» Say the sentence another way.
» Ask what was misunderstood.
» Correct your words.

Research on cooperative learning has identified characteristics of effective group language learning.

A first characteristic is that activities are structured such that there is a specific goal, product, or outcome for the collaboration. A group instruction to "discuss what makes children grow" is unlikely to lead to collaboration that is beneficial for language growth. A more effective approach is as follows:

> A lesson on comparatives (–er, –est) is embedded in a meaningful science lesson that begins with the teacher's oral reading of a selection on what influences children's growth. After the reading, the children measure their height. Each adds his or her height measurement to a graph and says, "I am taller than ____ and shorter than ____." Children divided into groups might be asked to arrange themselves in a row from tallest to shortest with a sentence using "I am taller than____." The lesson might continue with children comparing hand sizes or hair length and constructing graphs requiring everyone's input. A discussion on evidence could be included as well.

Teaching Practice 8: Provide structured interaction with peers that will require children to practice and communicate with others using the target form.

A second characteristic of effective collaboration is that each child's participation must be necessary and an individual-response process created so that each child has both an opportunity and expectation to contribute. One way to structure opportunity and expectation for participation is to have group roles of recorder, summarizer, question asker, and refocuser. Children can be given a card at the beginning of the collaboration that identifies their role. They need instruction and practice to learn these roles. There should be pauses in the collaboration for each person to perform his or her role.

Teaching Practice 9: Structure collaborative groups to have a specific goal and procedures that ensure each child's opportunity and responsibility to participate.

A third feature of effective collaborative groups is that children are grouped with others they like. This grouping practice increases the amount of interaction, support, and engagement among children. Grouping with "friendlies" generally supports rather than detracts from learning. Figure 4.5 describes a lesson on prepositions that includes student collaboration in the form of peer-partner activities.

Teaching Practice 10: Form groups where children who are friends can sometimes be together.

Student collaboration that best promotes children's mastery of English language structure will keep the language structure goals at the forefront. When all children of varying levels of English are outputting the language forms to be learned, creating discourse, checking for understanding, providing optimal input for others, and collaborating and helping along fellow travelers on the English language structure journey, then the journey is magical. And to think that you can make it happen . . .

Teaching Practice 11: Form groups that include children with differing levels of English proficiency, and provide ways for participation that are leveled according to their proficiency.

CHALLENGES FOR TEACHERS IN TEACHING LANGUAGE STRUCTURE

Educational Principle 2: Ensure that teachers have extensive knowledge of language structure, including phonology, morphology, syntax, and semantics.

Educational Principle 3: Provide teachers with effective, carefully selected curricula and instructional resources for teaching language structure.

There are several reasons that teachers of EBs are likely to need extensive support such as professional development, collaborative teacher study groups, or new high-quality curriculum materials to ensure that EBs learn English language structure. First, teachers' and researchers' estimates of language knowledge confirm that many teachers have limited knowledge and confidence about teaching language structure, particularly phonology, morphology, and syntax (see Moats, 2015, for review). Teachers may have inadequate education in learning about English language structure in teacher preparation programs (Joshi, Binks, Graham, Ocker-Dean, Smith, & Boulware-Gooden, 2009). Finally, language structure is comprised of an extraordinary level of detailed, technical, and complex attributes. Instruction that will lead to gains in EBs' proficiency with language form is very dependent upon teachers having an accurate and in-depth knowledge of phonology, morphology, syntax, and semantics. We will consider the issue of teacher knowledge again in Chapter 5.

Figure 4.5. Example of Form-Focused Lesson on Prepositions

Explain that the language form of the lesson is prepositions (form-focus): "Prepositions are words that tell about where something is."

Introduce a cardboard box and a vegetable and the group of words *in, on, above, below, under,* and *beside* as you place the vegetable in each location (form-focus). Ask the children to repeat with you (elicitation of form). Then show a photograph taken during a recent trip to the farmer's market that shows a sales stall with various fruits and vegetables displayed. Discuss what you saw and learned at the market and the differences between fruits and vegetables (discourse and science content meaning).

Have half the children draw a picture of a stall and all the fruits they saw and have the other half draw a stall showing all the vegetables they saw. Then have each child describe to a partner where they placed the fruit or vegetables using the words *in, on, below, above,* and *beside,* and have the partner draw what the other student describes (output practice).

Children discuss, using prepositions, each of their drawings and the original drawing, with correction of the use of the prepositions (output practice, correction).

Have each partner team agree on a sentence to tell how many fruits and vegetables were *on* something, *in* something, or *beside* something (shared goal and required contribution).

Use a sentence frame to scaffold for proficiency level, if needed:

There were ____ in a box. There were ______ kinds of fruit/vegetables under the table. And so forth.

THE PREK–GRADE 2 CONTINUUM: LEARNING LANGUAGE STRUCTURE

Educational Principle 4: Ensure that any English language development program selected and enacted in classrooms includes an explicit developmental sequence of language structure for phonology, morphology, and syntax.

The learning and use of English language structure begins orally in PreK. As children become more proficient readers in grades K–2, increasing amounts of text will be used for learning language structure. Spontaneous language use of PreK children and other novices will typically consist of one- to two-word utterances. Older children will speak longer utterances that communicate more complex meaning. They will also use more varied morphology, syntax, and semantics. All along the way, children will continue to make errors in language structure. Instruction that is geared to their level of English proficiency is important because teaching structure that is too distant from children's current developmental level is unlikely to be learned. None of us would think you could successfully teach algebra to a baby. Similarly, you cannot teach subordinate clauses to a 3-year-old English novice. An effective ELD program

Figure 4.6. Pre-K Simple Discourse Example

Teacher introduces a photograph of a child in the class.
Teacher models use of auxiliary verb *is*:

1. ***This is Kao Lee (shows photograph).***
2. How old are you, Kao Lee? ***She is __ years old.***
3. What is my name? Kao Lee is in (teacher name) preschool room.
4. ***She is happy when*** _____ (show photos on the picture board of Kao Lee such as riding bikes, eating a healthy item, playing house, or on the swing set. Have her point [novice], name [more English], or create her own response [most English]).

Teacher says: We will talk more about friends in our room. We will say *is* when we talk and tell things about friends.

Hand children a photo of a friend and have them repeat with the teacher or have children say to a partner the three example sentences shown in italics.

Scaffold for different proficiency levels and correct as needed.

will include a scope and sequence of the developmental progression of language form so that teachers know what may be within children's learning zone.

Discourse (several connected chunks of language in stories or informational text) may be comprised of only three to four sentences in PreK and may include several pages of text by grade 2. An example of a PreK lesson to teach the form *is* embedded in meaningful discourse is shown in Figure 4.6.

CONNECTIONS TO THE COMMON CORE STATE STANDARDS AND PRESCHOOL LEARNING STANDARDS

Typically, preschool learning foundations have limited specificity about language structure. For example, the Head Start language framework identifies two broad standards related to language structure: comprehending and using different forms of language and different grammatical structures (see Table 4.1). These elements tell teachers very little about what they should teach or monitor for progress. The Head Start standard on storytelling and engaging in conversation recognizes the importance of language discourse.

The CCSS contain double the number of learning outcomes for language structure compared with the average in preexisting state standards (Porter, McMaken, Hwang, & Yang, 2011). The elements of language structure for K–2 within the CCSS are reasonably consistent with the developmental sequence for acquisition of language structure. Table 4.2 summarizes the elements of the CCSS most related to language structure. There is also significant emphasis within the CCSS on speaking.

Table 4.1. Head Start Framework for Preschool Children's Language Development

Receptive Language	Expressive Language
• Attends to language such as conversations, songs, and stories • Comprehends increasingly complex and varied vocabulary • Comprehends forms such as questions and exclamations • Comprehends different grammatical structures or rules	• Communicates and converses with others • Expresses ideas and needs • Uses increasingly complex and varied vocabulary • Uses different forms of language • Uses different grammatical structures • Engages in storytelling and conversation

The sharply increased emphasis on language structure and language production has real potential to benefit EBs to the degree that it is accompanied by excellent instruction on those standards. The reading, speaking, and listening standards within the CSSS emphasize using language for academic learning. Academic language is dependent upon competence with language structure. In sum, EBs' growth in competence with English language structure has the potential to add to speaking and listening, and to academic language competence.

There are challenges for EBs within the CCSS. One limitation is that the standards refer primarily to word- and sentence-level structure. This chapter emphasized the benefits of embedding instruction on language structure within discourse. A discourse instructional approach will strengthen (1) children's competence with English language structure, and (2) their subject-matter, academic thinking and their communicative language learning. It is a two-for-one deal that can't be turned down. Discourse-level skills of argumentation, presentation, using evidence, and so on that are emphasized in the Common Core can grow when language form is taught while children are using language discourse. Finally, there are no CCSS related to phonology, with the possible exception of the standard that children's speech be audible. This is a significant omission.

Apply Your Knowledge: Examine a recent ELD lesson on language structure that you have taught. Identify the language form(s) focused upon. Is the language form related to those CCSS or other state standards specified for your grade level (K-grade 2) or within your oral language standards (PreK)? What do you conclude about the lesson?

Table 4.2. Kindergarten–Grade 2 Common Core Standards for Language

	Comprehension and Collaboration	Presentation of Knowledge and Ideas	Knowledge of Language	Conventions of Standard English
Kindergarten	Participate in collaborative conversations about kindergarten topics and texts: peers, adults, large, small groups	Describe familiar people, places, things, and events; with prompting, add detail	Begins in grade 2	Use common nouns and verbs; form regular plural nouns
Grade 1	Same as K, plus build upon others' ideas	Same, plus express the ideas above freely and clearly		Use common, proper, and possessive nouns
Grade 2	Same as K, plus build upon others' ideas		Use knowledge of language and conventions for reading, writing, speaking, and listening; compare formal and informal English	Use collective nouns; use irregular plural nouns
Kindergarten	Follow agreed-upon rules for discussion	Speak audibly and express ideas and feelings clearly		
Grade 1	Same as K			Use singular and plural nouns with verbs; use verbs for past, present, and future
Grade 2	Same as K			Use past tense of irregular verbs
Kindergarten	Continue a conversation			Understand and use question words
Grade 1	Same as K			
Grade 2	Same as K			
Kindergarten	Confirm comprehension: Ask and answer questions, request clarification			Use most frequently occurring prepositions
Grade 1	Same as K			Use common adjectives

Table 4.2. Continued

	Comprehension and Collaboration	Presentation of Knowledge and Ideas	Knowledge of Language	Conventions of Standard English
Grade 2	Same as K			Correctly use adjectives and adverbs
Kindergarten	Describe people, places, and things, and with support, provide more detail; add drawings or visuals to descriptions			Produce and expand complete sentences
Grade 1	Same, plus produce complete sentences			Produce and expand simple and compound declarative, interrogative, imperative, and exclamatory sentences
Grade 2	Same, plus recount key ideas or detail from oral or written text			Rearrange complete simple and complex sentences
Kindergarten	Improve comprehension with questions to seek help, get information, or clarify by questioning			
Grade 1	Same, plus questions to clear up confusion			Use common adjectives
Grade 2	Same, plus questions to deepen understanding			Correctly use adjective and adverbs
Kindergarten	Use drawings and media to add detail		Compare formal and informal uses of English	
Grade 1	Same			Use personal, possessive, and indefinite pronouns
Grade 2	Same, plus clarify meaning			Use reflexive pronouns

Educational Principles From Chapter 4

1. Develop instructional programs that include explicit and regular goals for teaching EBs the structure of the English language (phonology, morphology, syntax, and semantics).
2. Ensure that teachers have extensive knowledge of language structure, including phonology, morphology, syntax, and semantics.
3. Provide teachers with effective, carefully selected curricula and instructional resources for teaching language structure.
4. Ensure that any English language development program selected and enacted in classrooms includes an explicit developmental sequence of language structure for phonology, morphology, and syntax.

Teaching Practices from Chapter 4

1. Provide daily instruction in the sound structure (phonology), word structure (morphology), sentence structure (syntax), and semantic structure (vocabulary and discourse) of English.
2. Teach children how to correctly produce English phonemes.
3. Teach children the morphological rules for how to modify word structure to indicate past and present tense, comparatives, plurals, meanings associated with prefixes and suffixes, and other aspects of morphology consistent with their level of English language proficiency.
4. Teach children the syntactic rules for how to structure simple sentences and how to combine and embed sentences.
5. Limit the number of language forms to learn to one to two per lesson.
6. Teach language structure while children engage in extended, connected, and meaningful discourse.
7. Favor correction that elicits the correct language form and repetition of it while maintaining a stance as a collaborative partner.
8. Provide structured interaction with peers that will require children to practice and communicate with others using the target form.
9. Structure collaborative groups to have a specific goal and procedures that ensure each child's opportunity and responsibility to participate.
10. Form groups where children who are friends can sometimes be together.
11. Form groups that include children with differing levels of English proficiency, and provide ways for participation that are leveled according to their proficiency.

CHAPTER 5

Developing Foundations for Literacy

Alphabetic Knowledge, Phonemic Awareness, and Word Reading

Important Research Findings About Alphabetic Knowledge, Phonemic Awareness, and Word Reading

- The essential task in learning to read words is to tie together phonemes in spoken language with graphemes in printed language.
- Alphabetic knowledge and phonological awareness are the two best predictors of early reading ability, including comprehension.
- Children with limited English proficiency can learn alphabet letter names and sounds, phonemic awareness, and how to decode words in English.
- Explicit and high-quality instruction increases learning the alphabet, phonological awareness, and word reading.
- High-level comprehension is dependent upon word reading skill.
- Word reading efficiency is dependent upon extensive opportunity to read.
- Teacher knowledge and skill related to the structure of language and its relationship to early reading instruction influences learning to read and may be overestimated.

Most children have a basic and effective oral language system when they begin preschool. That effective language may be English or another language. Children skillfully use language to plan activities; to express their observations, wonderings, and desires; to negotiate; and to manage day-to-day activities. And there are those magic moments when they use language in such a unique, poetic, amusing, charming, or imaginative way that we adults are stopped in our tracks and say "wow." This basic and effective language system develops in all typical children worldwide, regardless of opportunity for schooling. The ability to acquire and manipulate oral language is an incredible endowment of the human species.

The ability to acquire and manipulate printed language—to be literate—is a more privileged acquisition that is not biologically endowed. It is dependent upon opportunities to see print, to attend to print, and to have adults who understand the relationship between speech and print explain it. Literacy does not develop in all typical children worldwide. It is a cultural endowment that is dependent upon the skill of a teacher.

In this chapter, I will explain the three foundations essential for learning to read print well. To read print well means to be able to decode the print accurately and quickly in order to obtain an oral pronunciation of each word, word after word, line after line, page after page. When children can decode accurately and quickly, mental space is freed up to discover and build the new knowledge and expressions of life provided in text.

Three essential foundations for learning to read well are alphabetic knowledge, phonemic awareness (PA), and word decoding (Roberts, 2011). Each of these topics could rightfully take a full semester or year of study to just learn the basics. You may even exclaim, "No, it was at least a year or 2 into teaching before I began to feel comfortable with beginning reading instruction." The scope of this chapter is necessarily very limited. I will explain why accurate and fast alphabetic, phonemic, and word reading skill is so important for EBs' skilled reading, and why a significant amount of carefully sequenced instruction delivered by teachers with deep and accurate knowledge of the English language and its representation in text is absolutely essential. I will explain both the nature of children's learning in each foundation and the instructional practices that are aligned with it. Some of you may object that "word calling" is not reading. Agreed. But it is a foundation that enables children to orchestrate the printed phonemes, word parts, words, and sentences in such a way that text meaning can be accessed and constructed into the symphony that is reading.

A goal of this chapter is to help you fully appreciate the value of extensive word reading practice through independent reading of text that beginning readers can and want to read. I hope to inspire a commitment to making the time each and every day for children to do the very thing we are all striving for from reading instruction: read with ease, pleasure, engagement, and mind-expanding learning.

THE PROCESS OF LEARNING TO READ

Steps in the Process

Mastering the relationship between oral language and print is the fundamental task in learning to read. The first step toward this mastery is to learn the many connections between individual elements of speech (phonemes or sounds) and individual elements of print (graphemes or alphabet letters). Each phoneme and letter (and eventually, sets of letters) must become tightly stitched together. The second and

Figure 5.1. The Process of Learning to Read

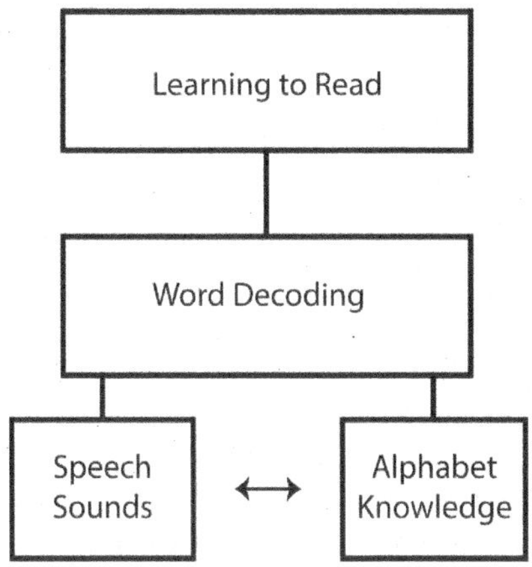

equally important step is to apply this well-learned knowledge of individual speech-to-print connections to reading printed words. A beginning reader must segment the printed word into a complete set of individual speech sounds and then quickly recombine, or blend, all of those sounds together in a manner to arrive at a whole correct word. The segmenting and blending step is called word decoding. Word decoding is necessary for accessing meaning. If children encounter the word *hog* in the sentence "The hog was very large," and cannot figure out through decoding the word"hog," they may think there was a large *log*, *dog*, or *bog*. Figure 5.1 shows the foundations of the learning to read process.

The Process for EBs

Educational Principle 1: Establish a strong emphasis on teaching the alphabet, phonemic awareness, and word decoding from PreK through grade 2.

There is now a convincing amount of research showing that EBs learn to read English using the same basic processes as are used by children whose first language is English (Nassaji, 2014). In addition, there is strong evidence that English learners can learn English alphabetic, phonemic awareness, and decoding foundations even when they have limited English proficiency (reviewed in Roberts, Christo, & Shefelbine, 2010). Reading instruction can proceed in tandem with oral language acquisition. EBs' level of alphabetic and phonemic awareness competence predicts not only word reading skills but also comprehension (Lesaux & Siegel, 2003). When EB preschool children sing the alphabet song, learn the first letter in their name, or hold up a letter card and chant the letter sound, they are learning reading foundations as surely as the 2nd-grade EB who practices decoding words with prefixes such as *unbutton* and *unhappy* (but not *under*!) or two-syllable words like *spider* and *paper.*

But this does not mean that learning the alphabet, phonemic awareness, and word decoding is exactly equivalent in nature or required effort for English fluent (EF) children and EBs. English fluent children know the meaning and pronunciations of many of the words they will be asked to decode. Thus, for EF children, the major task is to decode the print. EB children on the other hand, have a twofold task. Jacqueline, a 1st-grader whose first language is Spanish, must learn to decode print while she is simultaneously acquiring oral English. This will make the foundational learning more demanding for her, compared to Elizabeth, who is a native speaker of English.

Skilled word decoding (accurate and fast) can release mental resources for comprehending. EBs' reading comprehension is highly related to their word reading skill (Geva, Yaghoub-Zadeh, & Schuster, 2000; Lesaux & Siegel, 2003). Furthermore, for EBs who are struggling readers, like their EF counterparts, managing the phonological demands of word decoding is the major difficulty (Geva, Yaghoub-Zadeh, & Schuster, 2000). In short, improving the English oral proficiency of EBs without simultaneously ensuring strong decoding ability will leave learners without the tools to efficiently draw upon that oral proficiency. If children cannot decode the words, they will certainly not be able to comprehend, no matter how good their vocabulary, reasoning, strategic thinking, and world knowledge might be. The text will be impenetrable for them.

The look at the beginning to read process we have just completed identifies that EBs need all of the following:

- The ability to separate words in speech into individual phonemes (phonemic awareness)
- The knowledge of the letters that stand for each of those sounds (alphabet knowledge)
- The skill to accurately and quickly break printed words into phonemes and recombine these phonemes to arrive at an accurate word pronunciation (word decoding)

We can say with confidence that the steps shown in Figure 5.1 also pertain to EBs.

For a skilled reader, these three skills become so well interleaved and quickly executed that it can be challenging to step back to the basics and see how large a task it is for a beginner. And it is even more demanding for EBs, to the extent that their

> *Apply Your Knowledge:* A very good way to consolidate learning and to evaluate your own learning is to explain it to yourself. Explain the basic reading process you have just read and record your explanation into your phone or another recording device. Now, listen to it. What does your rendition tell you about teaching reading foundations? This exercise would be good practice for explaining the learning to read process to teaching assistants or families.

knowledge of English is limited. Impeccably effective instruction is needed. We will look next at the teaching principles and lesson examples that apply in PreK–2 for teaching alphabetic knowledge, phonemic awareness, and word reading.

GENERAL PRINCIPLES FOR TEACHING THE ALPHABET, PHONEMIC AWARENESS, AND WORD READING

Teaching Practice 1: Teach reading foundations appropriate for children's developmental level to EBs of all levels of English proficiency.

It is useful that there is a set of seven instructional principles supported by research that are effective for teaching all three of the foundational skills to EBs. Although some believe that very special and unique instruction is necessary to meet the learning and psychological needs of preschool children, the following seven principles for teaching reading foundations are applicable in PreK–2:

1. *Instruction should be explicit and structured.* Explicit instruction has a specific goal that is shared with children—even preschoolers. Children are told: "The lesson for today is to hear the sound /h/ at the beginning of words." The instructional routines and learner activities to achieve that goal are preplanned. Explicit instruction is largely teacher-directed, with teachers clearly explaining important points to children. Explicit instruction is such an important feature of high-quality instruction in reading foundations that I devote the next section to explain its benefits.
2. *Activities and teaching must stay focused on the instructional goal.* Imagine a teacher who is delivering a PA lesson on the phoneme /b/ using the word *bug* for detecting the /b/ sound. A child reports, "Hey, we had ants in our garbage." It is very tempting for a teacher to say, "And what did you do about those ants? I have ants at my house, too." From there, a discussion ensues about household pests. The focus on the goal has been blurred, and time has been allocated to purposes other than the goal. As a result, there will be less learning of the phoneme /b/.
3. *Each PreK–2 lesson should focus on only one to two related skills.* For example, a PA lesson (remember that this begins as an oral skill) in a comprehensive PreK "boxed" curriculum asked children to listen for the sound /d/ at the beginning and end of several words while "sky writing" the letter, to find and mark letter *d* on a practice page, to generate words that began with letter d and to identify the names of classmates that started with /d/. There are too many different letters and too many different concepts all at once!
4. *There should be many opportunities for practice and repetition.* When children learn to write the letter O, four to six practice attempts on a whiteboard will help consolidate the muscle movements required.

5. *Children's learning will be honed by speaking targeted learning.* Oral speaking supports the accurate learning of letter names and sounds by utilizing the concrete information that speaking provides. It also provides children with feedback on the accuracy of their vocalizations.
6. *Lessons or follow-up activities must demonstrate to children the real-world and personal usefulness of print, phonemic awareness, and word decoding.* For younger children, labeling things and finding letters in personal names and print associated with familiar routines such as daily sign-in and tooth brushing are examples. For older children, the most direct route to meaningfulness and personal usefulness is selecting and reading books at a decoding level consistent with what they have been taught and can read.
7. *Effective instruction in reading foundations helps children engage, persevere, and seek challenge.* This principle is very important for EBs, who typically have to work very hard to simultaneously learn both the print and the language it represents.

Figure 5.2 shows a series of questions to guide lesson planning for teaching alphabetic knowledge, PA, and word reading goals based on these seven principles.

Teaching Practice 2: Plan lessons that explicitly state the learning goal, maintain that focus, teach no more than one to two skills, provide ample practice, involve oral participation, extend lesson content to meaningful and authentic use, and support children's engagement.

WHY EXPLICIT INSTRUCTION IN READING FOUNDATIONS IS NECESSARY

Imagine that you are an English-speaking 5-year-old student and have been in a kindergarten where Hindi is the language of instruction for just a few days. You did not go to preschool. All of the adults in the room speak a language you do not understand. You look around at the other children and try to do what they do; they move to the carpet and you follow along. The teacher passes out small books to everyone and she has a large one just like it. Some children open their books and you do the same, just a few seconds behind. She writes on the board a sentence in Hindi:

मुझे पढ़ना पसंद है

Next, the teacher points at these marks and says something. You hear one word that you know in this strange language, *I*. She reads again, but no matter how carefully you listen to all of the little bits of language and watch the print, you are bewildered. You notice that other children are now pointing to these marks in their book and saying some of the same sounds the teacher made. You look around and see that the other English-speaking children you played with on the playground this morning seem as lost as you are. You make funny faces together and tlaugh. Take a moment

Figure 5.2. Explicit Alphabet, Phonemic Awareness, and Word Decoding Lesson Plan Outline

1. What will you tell children is the goal of the lesson (one to two skills only)?
2. How will you include practice and repetition of the letter, phoneme, or word reading skill?
3. How will you make sure that all children orally participate with accurate speaking of the letters, phonemes, or words being decoded?
4. How will you make sure children are attending to print for alphabet learning and word decoding?
5. How will you incorporate self-regulated, meaningful, and personally useful opportunities (for example, reading self-selected books, writing on self-selected topics, dramatic play, science, math, art, classroom routines) to use the alphabetic, phonemic awareness, or word reading skill you have taught?
6. What will you do to promote positive motivation?

---

to answer the question: What would you ask this teacher to do to help you figure out the marks and the words that go with them?

It is highly likely that you would want the teacher to figure out a way to explain to you what you are trying to do—the goal of the lesson. She will have to be very clever in using gestures, pictures, examples, and demonstrations so that you can understand the words. You would want her to explain that those little bits of print go with the words she is saying, in a pattern. You would want her to explain the pattern—which little bits of print go with exactly which bits of language. And you would want her to explain it again, because no matter how hard you listen, those little bits of speech go by very quickly! You would probably want her to explain these things several times and to give you lots of opportunities to practice how the little bits go with the words. A set of little colored tiles with individual print bits written on them could help you learn what those bits look like and keep track of the speech bits they "go with." At the end, you would really like to have some time where you can explore, study, and practice with the little book on your own or maybe with a partner. You would want the teacher to tell you when you had it right and to help you where you were uncertain in such a way that the next time you would feel confident enough to figure it out on your own. You hope that the next time she teaches this or a related lesson, she will pass out the books and tell about the bits of speech and the bits of print in just the same way and in the same order. You just might be able to hang on if you can anticipate what comes next in each lesson. And you would really, really want her to know how very hard you are trying. When the teacher does all this, and adds in a smile and patience, a foreigner is transformed into a partner, and maybe even a friend. And in the end, when you can learn how to connect the speech and print bits to read the sentence "I like to read," you will really mean it.

I hope this vignette has helped you appreciate the myriad and complex knowledge and skill that is needed to master reading foundations and why explicit instruction is more effective than other practices. Charles, a kindergartener, may discover that heavier items sink faster than lighter ones at the water table. But he will not be able to unlock the speech-to-print relationship of reading by exploring a print-rich environment, listening to storybook reading, or pointing out print in the environment like restaurant signs, labels on cereal boxes, and the like.

A critical piece of the explicit instruction package is a curriculum that offers robust, accurate, engaging, and sequential instructional routines to support you, the teacher, in teaching reading foundations. I, for one, would consider it a daunting task to decide each day what I should teach based on a scientifically identified developmental sequence, to find the exemplar words, to create all the child-engaging activities, to develop practice and independent exercises, and to locate books that I was confident would help children of varying levels practice their newly learned decoding skills. How children learn each of the three essential reading foundations and the specific features of instruction that will draw upon and strengthen this learning are detailed in the next section.

HOW CHILDREN LEARN READING FOUNDATIONS WITH EFFECTIVE TEACHING PRACTICES

Educational Principle 2: Provide teachers and their students a rich set of materials with which to teach the three essential foundations.

A Key to the Castle: Knowing the Language Used in Reading Foundations Instruction

The language used to teach the alphabet, phonemic awareness, and word reading must be taught. Children cannot identify the first sound when they don't understand the meaning of *first* or *sound.* They cannot stretch the sounds in the word *kick* if they don't understand what it means to *stretch.* They can't use the word *slant* to guide writing the letter *M* if they do not understand it. Figure 5.3 identifies many of these words. Are there other words you regularly use while teaching reading foundations? If so, pencil them in on the list. It can take some ingenuity to figure out how to teach these words.

Teaching Practice 3: Teach children the meaning of the words regularly used to teach the alphabet, phonemic awareness, and word reading.

The Alphabet

Learning. Knowledge of written alphabet letters, or graphemes, is the major building block for the print element of the speech-to-print process that is fundamental to word reading. Children must learn to recognize and distinguish 26 upper-

Figure 5.3. Words Used During Alphabet, Phonemic Awareness, and Word Reading Instruction

- **Alphabet:** *word, name, sound, letter, first, last, listen, say, down, up, across,*
- *around, slant*
- **Phonemic awareness:** *sound, first, last, put together, take apart, mouth, lips, throat, tongue, teeth, air*
- **Decoding:** *word, first, last, middle, sound, letter, name, blend, segment, pair, team, syllable, beginning, ending, stretch, vowel, sentence*

case and 26 lowercase letters (16 are similar to uppercase ones) and learn how the 44 individual phonemes in spoken English map onto these letters. Those mappings combine together to make words. Pause and think about it—26 uppercase letters, 26 lowercase letters, 44 phonemes. That is a very large learning space. And children will need to know all of these connections to read accurately. One missing piece of correct information can change a *bat* into a *hat*!

Children learn this extensive and complex set of connections between a letter name/sound and the grapheme that stands for it by using a basic process of human thinking called *paired-associate learning*. This connection-making process is difficult when one letter looks or sounds like another. It is also difficult when a child does not have a clear image of the details of the printed form. For example, the difference between letter shapes *F* and *E* or *M* and *N* can be quite subtle to a beginner's eye. Letters that have the letter sound at the beginning of the letter name (*B*, *K*, *T*) are easier to learn than letters with the letter sound at the end (*M*, *F*). Say these letter names out loud and listen to whether your mouth forms the letter sound at the beginning or end of the letter name. Letters at the beginning and the end of the alphabet are learned better than those in the middle. Remember that famous old kindergarten letter LMNOP? Uppercase letters are easier to learn than lowercase letters. Some of these characteristics are shown in Table 5.1.

Teaching Practice 4: Carefully plan the sequence of letter instruction to take into account letter difficulty and ensure that children do not confuse letters.

Teaching Practice 5: Teach the complete alphabet.

Teaching. The previous discussion of how children learn to connect letter names/sounds with written letters leads directly to several teaching practices:

- Have the children repeat and practice saying each letter shape–name/sound correspondence to tightly and securely stitch together the letter shapes and their names/sounds.
- Focus attention on the visual elements of each letter shape and how to discriminate each letter from others.
- Ensure accurate pronunciation of the letter name or letter sound.

Table 5.1. Characteristics of Letters That Influence Learning

Letter	Easily Confused letter shape	Confusable letter sound	Letter sound at beginning of letter name	Letter sound at end of letter name	Letter sound not in letter name	Letter name in long vowel
A*						X
B	d, p, q, g	d, p, t	X			
C		s	X			
D	b, p, q, g	b, p, t	X			
E*						X
F		v		X		
G		j	X			
H					X	
I*						X
J		g	X			
K		t	X			
L				X		
M		n		X		
N		m		X		
O*						X
P	b, d, q, g	b, d	X			
Q	b, d, q, g				X	
R				X		
S		z		X		
T		p, d	X			
U*						X
V		b, f	X			
W					X	
X				X		
Y		i			X	
Z		s	X			

*The letters *A*, *E*, *I*, *O*, and *U* have letter names based on the sound used when they are long vowels, in words such as *play*, *sneeze*, *mice*, *hose*, and *huge*.

Apply Your Knowledge: Respond to these reflective questions:

1. Based on what you have learned, why might "sky writing," where the child is instructed to write the letter in the air with his or her hand, be ineffective for learning letter names, sounds, or shapes?
2. Why might children's ability to write their name or to say the names of the letters in their name be a weak indicator of alphabet knowledge?
3. Why might it be a good idea to have PreK children learn to write their name with uppercase letters?

> ***Apply Your Knowledge:*** Study the uppercase and lowercase letters. What reasons can you think of for why the uppercase ones are easier to learn? Hint: Compare the letters in the top and bottom lines one by one.
>
> A B C D E F G H I J K L M N O P Q R S T U V W X Y Z
> a b c d e f g h i j k l m n o p q r s t u v w x y z

My colleague Patricia Vadasy and I recently designed preschool alphabet instruction in which each lesson began with children being told the specific name or sound that was the goal of the lesson. Next, children repeated the target name or sound for a letter card that was slowly drawn out from a "special delivery" envelope. We also drew children's attention to how the letter name or letter sound was spoken (articulated) to support accurate pronunciation. We taught children the words *lips, tongue, teeth, throat, nose,* and *air,* followed by children using small mirrors to watch their mouths as they articulated names or sounds. We taught children to write letters and to name the visual features of letters (*slant, up, down, across, around*) as they were writing. We taught this vocabulary for speaking sounds and describing letter writing to benefit EBs and other children who may not have known these words. Lessons ended with a self-regulated game in which children discriminated between the letter they had last learned, the letter currently being learned, and the next letter to be learned. The lessons lasted no more than 10–12 minutes. This type of instruction led to superior alphabet learning, compared with instruction that did not include these routines. (See Figure 5.4 for a "feed the bear" game used in the study for discriminating the letter *B*.)

To summarize, materials to enhance alphabet learning include the following:

- Pictures of mouth movements for letter names or sounds
- Small mirrors
- Whiteboards or primary paper for letter writing
- Alphabet books with distinctive letters and fonts

Practices for comparing and contrasting letter shapes are as follows:

- Writing letters while describing their visual features (letter *F*: down, across, across)
- Comparing two to three taught letters to one another (how are the letters *S* and *M* the same and different?)

> ***Apply Your Knowledge:*** Review the seven principles of instruction presented earlier in the chapter. Go back through the lesson just described and identify how each principle is implemented. One of the principles is missing. Which one is it?

Figure 5.4. Letter B Discrimination Game

Children close their eyes, mix up the little letter cards, open their eyes, find the target letter *B*, and feed it to the bear. This game was played three to four times every day with a different animal whose initial letter sound corresponded to the target letter. The children never tired of it.

- Sorting letters according to around, across, slant features (*E*, *F*, *T* across; *S*, *B*, *O* around)

Teaching Practice 6: Model and teach children to accurately pronounce letter names and letter sounds.

Teaching Practice 7: Provide a lot of practice and repetition in pairing the letter name/sound with the letter shape.

Teaching Practice 8: Provide many opportunities for children to discriminate one letter from other letters.

Teaching Practice 9: Teach children to write the letters correctly.

A final aspect of effective alphabet learning is for children to experience the real-world and personal usefulness of alphabet letters. This may occur at the end of formal lessons where children look at personal names or alphabet books, construct a "b" page with pictures of words that begin with the letter name or sound *b*, or write a note on a topic that will encourage use of the letter to a family member. Letter activities can also be extended into centers, subject areas such as science and social studies, and classroom and digital print. Learning the meaningfulness of print will be promoted when children are using letters under their own volition and for their own purposes, such as writing notes, labeling drawings, and so on.

Apply Your Knowledge: Evaluate the materials or curriculum that you use to teach letter names and sounds. Answer the following questions:

- How effective is it for creating a strong stitching together of the verbal label and the grapheme?
- How effective is it for comparing and contrasting letter shapes?
- How effective is it for ensuring that children pronounce names or sounds accurately?
- How effective is it for helping children learn to write letters?
- How effective is it for helping children see and use letters in meaningful contexts?

Teaching Practice 10: Provide many opportunities for children to see and write letters for meaningful and real-world purposes.

Phonemic Awareness

Learning. Phonemic awareness is the ability to identify and manipulate individual phonemes in words. Children show a level of phonemic awareness that will support word reading when they can *orally* separate the word *dog* into the phonemes /d/ /o/ /g/ and when they can *orally* blend the phonemes /d/ /o/ /g/ together to form the word *dog*. I emphasize the word *orally* to help you keep in mind that PA lessons initially occur in the oral, not written, mode. Understanding that PA is an oral language skill will help you distinguish alphabet knowledge from PA competence. After children acquire extensive alphabet knowledge, phonemes and letters should be connected. Separating the individual phonemes in a word is different from what is done in natural oral language. In natural language, the phonemes are interleaved and strung together seamlessly. In natural language, attention is almost exclusively paid to meaning. In learning to read, the inclination to pay attention to meaning alone must be set aside. The individual phonemes must be noticed, paid attention to, and manipulated.

Teaching Practice 11: Use oral language, rather than print, for initial development of phonemic awareness.

Some curricula and learning standards focus on recognizing and generating rhymes (What is a word that rhymes with *hat*?), separating compound words (*butter-fly*), or counting syllables (*cat er pill ar*) as initial PA skills. These competencies with chunks of language bigger than phonemes are called *phonological awareness*. Yet, the National Reading Panel (NRP, 2000), in its review of scientifically rigorous research on PA, concluded that skill at the individual phoneme level was needed to learn to read well. The ability to say /h/ when asked, "What is the first sound in *hot?*" or to say /t/ when asked "What is the last sound in *hot?*" reveal phoneme-level competence. The NRP also found that preschool-age English-proficient children gained almost twice as much from phoneme-level instruction as did K–2 children, indicating that PA instruction is very appropriate for preschoolers.

Recent studies show that with high-quality and regular instruction, 4-year-olds, including EBs, can successfully name initial and sometimes final sounds in English words, and can separate and blend English words comprised of two to three phonemes. So, reach upward and onward with confidence that EBs can do it. Finally, if EBs have learned PA or to read efficiently in another language, teachers can expect that PA from L1 will transfer (Geva et al., 2000).

Teaching. The main goal of high-quality phonemic awareness instruction for EB children is to help them learn to separate and combine individual phonemes in words (Phillips, Menchetti, & Lonigan, 2008). Teaching practices to help EBs achieve this goal include the following:

- Focusing attention on word structure
- Using articulatory (mouth movement) cues
- Making phonemes concrete
- Using short, familiar words
- Teaching the vocabulary used in PA instruction

Individual lessons incorporating these practices while teaching only one to two PA skills will lend EBs a critical helping hand.

Because PreK–2 children are oriented to language meaning, their ability to stay focused on the sounds in the word—its structure—will require them to shift their attention away from meaning. Young children's ability to control their attention is far from fully developed. For this reason, frequent reminders to "listen to the little sounds" or to clap the sounds or count the sounds by moving little tiles will help children stay focused on word structure. Resisting the temptation to engage in meaning-based digressions during instruction will also help. For example, in a lesson where the word *bat* is used to listen for phoneme /b/, comments such as "Bats eat insects" will distract children from focusing on the initial sound /b/.

PA instruction that targets fewer tasks is more effective than PA instruction targeting several tasks in one lesson (National Reading Panel, 2000), likely because attention is more focused when there are fewer types of tasks.

Teaching Practice 12: Help children stay focused on word structure during phonemic awareness instruction.

Accurate, clear, and repeated oral pronunciation—by both teacher and child— of the individual phonemes that children are trying to hear, attend to, and identify will help each sound stand tall in children's minds. Mouth pictures of phonemes and small mirrors to use while children are saying sounds and words are also helpful. When a single sound is attended to and repeated several times, a clear idea of it will be deeply etched in children's minds. Progressive stretching of word pronunciations can help children hear the individual phonemes in whole words. Teachers can model slower and slower speaking of a word until each phoneme is detached and stands alone. Children repeat along with them. One-inch letter tiles can be used for each phoneme while children identify sounds, count sounds in words, or stretch sounds. The ability of teachers to accurately pronounce the individual phonemes in a consistent manner will help children in all this learning.

Apply Your Knowledge: Read the following list of materials to enhance phonemic awareness learning:

» Pictures of mouth movements for phonemes
» Small mirrors
» 1-inch tiles—some blank and some with letters
» Pictures of familiar, one-syllable words for identifying initial, final, and medial sounds
» Small sticks to tap out sounds
» Strips with boxes on them to use for counting phonemes

Identify one or two ways you could use each of these materials to help you teach phonemic awareness.

Individual phonemes are ephemeral and short-lived compared to whole spoken words. They literally take only milliseconds to pronounce. In natural speech, phonemes are tied together with neighboring ones. I liken this to a watercolor painting, where individual colors blend together. Instructional routines to help EBs separate these blended phonemes are a quintessential feature of PA instruction that will lead to children's ability to attend to and ultimately manipulate individual phonemes on their own. Various techniques have been used in instructional research to accomplish this separating of sounds: hand clapping, stick tapping, and moving small tiles with each spoken phoneme.

Teaching Practice 13: Make phonemes concrete by using manipulatives to represent them.

Teaching children to correctly articulate speech sounds enhances phonemic awareness (Boyer & Ehri, 2011). Drawing children's attention to how the speech apparatus produces (articulates) phonemes adds motoric information to their learning, thereby helping make phonemes concrete. Using a chart to depict the speech apparatus and how different sounds are made, and teaching the meaning of the words that describe speech production such as *tongue, throat,* and *lips,* will be helpful for EBs. Providing children with small mirrors again for further exploration of the phonemes targeted in PA lessons is helpful, too.

Teaching Practice 14: Make phonemes concrete by teaching the mouth movements to represent them.

Using common, one-syllable words comprised of two to four phonemes (*pig, boat, hi, dog, jump*) will make it easier for beginner EBs to find, remember, and pronounce the individual phonemes. These words are often referred to as "CV" (consonant-vowel), or "CVC" (consonant-vowel-consonant words). As PA skill grows, longer words can be included in instruction. Words that have blends (sounds that are closely tied to one another when they are pronounced) such as the /f/ and /r/ in the word *frog* should be avoided. There are websites, phonological awareness teaching resources, and curricula that provide lists of good words for teaching phonological awareness. Try googling "CVC words."

Teaching Practice 15: Select one-syllable, common words of two to three phonemes for initial phonemic awareness instruction.

Word Decoding

Learning. Word reading speed and accuracy is the third essential foundation for developing good comprehension and the ability to think and reason with text. Typically, when children hear the word *dog* spoken, they envision a four-legged creature and perhaps the very small white bichon they have at home. When beginning readers encounter the word *dog* in print, they must first convert the print to each of the phonemes /d/, /o/, /g/, and then reconnect them into a representation of a word in order to access the meaning of the little white bichon.

The ability to convert print to individual phonemes and then to recombine the phonemes to accurately detect a real word is the essence of decoding. Even if children have very good oral language, they cannot bypass print during reading. Without skill in word decoding, it will be impossible to comprehend well and to think and reason about text. I am sure you can appreciate that for EBs, compared to EF children, this is a more challenging task because EBs are learning both oral language *and* the print elements at the same time.

Gaps in children's knowledge of the speech elements (phonemes), the written elements (graphemes), or the connection of the two can lead to incomplete or burdensome word decoding. The consequences of inaccurate or incomplete speech and print knowledge can be illustrated with the sentence "The hog was very big." Think about what has gone awry when the child reads "The hog was very bad," or "The hat was very big," or "The hug was very big," or "The hug was very bag," or even "The hot was very bad."

Teaching. The goal of initial word decoding instruction for children is learning the consistent one-to-one spelling patterns that will enable them to quickly apply that knowledge to the reading of simplified texts such as "The cat sat." There is a bit of magic in going from saying /c/, /a/, /t/, to arriving at the blended word *cat.* A great deal of teacher oral modeling and guiding children in how to interleave the individual phonemes is needed. Children acquire an insight, drawn from their knowledge of oral language, about how individual phonemes can be combined to make words. For EBs, this insight into the magic of how to take individual sounds (/c/, /a/, /t/) and interleave them to form a word will likely take more practice and teacher attention because EBs have less knowledge of English words. One practice to help children acquire the blending insight is to use small magic wands (they can be simple colored chopsticks resembling a wand like those seen in the Harry Potter movies) that children use to tap and name each phoneme and then "do the magic" by quickly running the wand under each word as they as they pronounce it.

Extensive practice with decodable texts is very valuable. The purpose of decodable books is to help children secure their knowledge of phoneme-grapheme correspondences in memory, see the utility of word decoding thorough practicing it in real texts that yield meaning, and gain initial confidence in decoding. These decodable books have been criticized because they have less literary quality than other books. However, decodable books provide children with practice in reading words controlled for the decoding skills they have been taught. Ideally, children will quickly gain sufficient word decoding skill to unlock print and enter the wide world of enriched meaning that is available in other, child-selected books.

After the initial learning of simple one-to-one relationships and how to decode words comprised of them, the decoding process diversifies, and therefore, so does the instruction that children need. Eventually, children will need to learn the complete system for mapping the 44 phonemes of the English language to the 26 letters or letter combinations that represent them. These combinations should be explained and taught to children in a progression, going from easier to more complex and difficult patterns. After instruction, there should be opportunity for children to practice by reading, reading, reading.

A final component of effective decoding instruction is to teach children what to do when they cannot decode a word. The first line of attack should be to look more closely at the word, to examine each letter and word parts to determine what phonics knowledge might apply. The recommendation to "look at the pictures" or to "predict what word might make sense" is unlikely to reveal the actual word because the picture and the context are typically not sufficiently precise. (See Figure 5.5 for how to engage families in supporting their EB children in reading.)

Figure 5.5. How to Engage Families in Emergent Bilinguals' Learning Foundations for Literacy

- Before making home recommendations, determine the language children will learn to read in:
  - ✓ If English, and there are no fluent English speakers in the home, make sure that all home assignments can be accomplished by children on their own.
  - ✓ If first language, encourage families to talk about materials written in the first language, especially concepts of print (front, back, author, word, page) and how words are written.
- Help parents understand how to rhyme and clap, and switch and count the sounds in first language words.
- Help families learn where to find easy-to-read books.
- Help families figure out how to provide a quiet space and time for reading several times a week.
- Ask families to listen to their children read short amounts of English text that the children then explain in their first language.

Teaching Practice 16: Teach the complete system of grapheme-phoneme correspondences, beginning with those that consistently link one phoneme to one grapheme.

Teaching Practice 17: Provide children with extensive opportunities to read texts that are decodable with the word reading knowledge they have.

ACCURACY AND SPEED IN READING FOUNDATIONS

Word reading accuracy and speed are both critical for developing good comprehension. Precursor skills for word reading include alphabet knowledge and phonemic awareness. Please stop here for a moment and think about accuracy and speed in all three foundations. What happens when children are not accurate, when they mistake one letter for another, or when they say /b/ and the correct phoneme is /v/? The consequences of inaccuracy are fairly obvious, aren't they? But why does *speed* matter in all of these skills?

Many preschool and kindergarten teachers have been taught that "hurrying children up" creates negative conditions for learning and emotional well-being. However, children must decode print accurately and quickly and come up with an oral pronunciation of each word—word after word, line after line, page after page. When children can decode accurately and quickly, thinking space is freed up and the effort to discover and build the new knowledge and expressions of life contained in text is eased. Speed in performing foundational skills is an indication of deep learning. It is for this reason that progress monitoring of speed, such as rapid letter naming and word reading fluency, is important. These measures are not meant to equate with what a skilled reader can and should do to comprehend. Turning on the key to the car is not the same as driving it, but driving is dependent upon it.

Teaching Practice 18: Teach and assess for both accuracy and speed in all three foundational skills.

Teaching Practice 19: Respond to deficiencies in speed by determining why children are slowed and provide additional instruction and practice in the knowledge they need.

Teaching Practice 20: Provide children with extensive opportunities to read texts that are based on the word reading knowledge they have and that are interesting to them.

Having just explained why speed in letter naming, phonemic awareness, and word reading is important, I am going to qualify the idea of speed with respect to word reading fluency for EBs. There is reason to think that the fluency level needed by EBs to support reading comprehension may be different from that required for English fluent children. The following may slow reading fluency for EBs without necessarily reflecting the same word reading and comprehension difficulties associated with slowed fluency in EF children (Brown, 1998*):*

- Slower rates of second language production
- Less ability to rapidly make the mouth movements for English speech
- First language influences

Apply Your Knowledge: Reflect upon the question: Why is speed important for letter identification, phoneme identification, and word reading? Then consider the following possible reasons and number them from 1 (most important) to 4 (least important):

- » Speed helps children finish their tasks more quickly. __
- » Speed allows more of the heavily laden curriculum to be covered. __
- » Speed allows children to convert print to meaning more easily and efficiently. __
- » Speed shows that children have been paying attention and making good progress. __

CHALLENGES TEACHERS FACE IN TEACHING READING FOUNDATIONS

Educational Principle 3: Ensure that all teaching staff have accurate knowledge of the structure of English and how this applies to alphabetic, phonemic awareness, and word decoding instruction.

Many teachers have limitations in knowledge and usage of the structure of English. These limitations carry over into beginning reading instruction. Discussion of these challenges was included in Chapter 4. EBs are particularly dependent on having a teacher who understands English language structure and its relationship to reading foundations. They can ill afford to try to learn from a teacher who may not fully understand the very linguistics foundations they are trying to understand. Essential teacher knowledge and skill about language structure needed by all PreK–2 personnel involved in teaching reading foundations includes the following:

- Differentiating speech sounds from letters
- Accurately speaking English phonemes and words
- Detecting identity/number of phonemes in words
- Possessing knowledge of letter combinations for many phonemes
- Understanding spelling units, digraphs, blends, and silent letters
- Understanding syllable division and syllable spelling
- Knowing the linguistic components of a sentence
- Determining the nature of children's phonological, orthographic, and syntactic/morphological problems
- Understanding interrelatedness of print, speech, and word reading

THE PREK–GRADE 2 CONTINUUM: DEVELOPING FOUNDATIONS FOR LITERACY

Educational Principle 4: Use similar lesson plan rubrics and materials to support learning reading foundations from PreK through grade 2.

You have seen that there are many principles of instruction and supports for learning that effectively teach reading foundations across PreK–2. It would be enormously beneficial to EBs to experience a PreK–2 curriculum that is planned around these commonalities. Precursor competencies for word reading include alphabet knowledge and phonemic awareness. Preschool EBs can learn alphabet letter names and sounds and to identify the first and perhaps last phoneme in words when they are provided with high-quality and regular instruction. Lessons throughout PreK–2 based on the same seven principles listed earlier in the chapter would provide continuity, comfort, familiarity, and reduction in the effort needed by EBs to learn reading foundations. Also important are PreK–2 lessons that use similar routines and materials (such as articulation cues and pictures or concrete tiles for counting phonemes).

However, to establish continuity in reading foundations instruction will take an extended and effortful team approach across preschool and K–2 programs. What are some ways that you might get started in your programs? One way would be to ask a preschool teacher (if you are K–2) or a K–2 teacher (if you are preschool) to share the instructional materials used for teaching the alphabet or PA. Collegial

Figure 5.6. Developmental Progression of Reading Foundations

- Ages 2-3: concepts about print, rhyming, syllables, the alphabet song, introduction and recognition of letters
- Age 4: first sounds in oral words, many to all letter names and sounds, two-phoneme blending, reading very simple decodable text and pretend reading
- Kindergarten: complete alphabetical knowledge; initial, final, and medial sounds in oral words; phoneme segmentation and phoneme blending of simple words; extensive reading of books requiring mostly the phonics they have been taught
- Grade 1: reading simple words, blends, and spelling patterns; extensive reading of books requiring mostly the phonics they have been taught
- Grade 2: reading irregular words, multisyllable words, and word form variations (prefixes, suffixes)

collaboration between PreK and K–2 means that information and planning flow in both directions.

The foundational skills for reading and writing that are most important vary by developmental level. More advanced skills are generally dependent on less advanced skills. For example, the ability of 4- to 5-year-olds to blend simple words is dependent upon knowing letter sounds. Figure 5.6 shows what typical children, including EBs, of each age can do with high-quality instruction. There will be individual variation in the rate at which children acquire these skills, but level of English proficiency is not a reason by itself for slowed progress. It is time to call out again the importance of high expectations and high-quality instruction to provide EBs with the support they need to meet these age-appropriate expectations.

As children begin to acquire the ability to read independently using texts that allow them to put their growing print (orthography) and speech (phonemes) knowledge to work reading words (decoding), extensive reading to build the accuracy and speed with which they can connect print and speech as they occur in real texts is necessary. Practice at reading text that is too difficult can lead to discouragement, confusion, and low motivation. It also prevents children from acquiring the extensive practice they need to anchor word reading accuracy and speed.

CONNECTIONS TO THE COMMON CORE STATE STANDARDS AND PRESCHOOL LEARNING STANDARDS

The emphasis on foundational skills has decreased in the Common Core era compared to what was present in earlier literacy reforms. It will be very detrimental for EBs if this decreased attention leads to neglect of foundational skills. Foundational skills are even more important when children are asked to think critically, read complex text, and perform close reading. Accuracy and speed in word reading free

Table 5.2. Common Core Standards for Reading Foundations K–2

Print concepts	Phonological awareness (oral)	Phonics and Word Reading (print)	Fluency
KINDERGARTEN			
Understands organization and features of print left to right, top to bottom, page-by-page Words are represented by letters and spaces Recognizes and names uppercase letters	Knows words, syllables, and sounds Produces rhyming words Blends/segments: syllables, onset/rimes Identifies initial, medial, and final sounds Adds/substitutes sounds	Knows sounds of frequent consonants Long/short sounds for 5 vowels High-frequency sight words Identifies sounds of letters that differ in words	Reads emergent reader texts
1ST GRADE			
Same, plus recognizes sentences	Knows words, syllables, and sounds Distinguishes long/short vowels in spoken words Orally blends one-syllable words Pronounces initial, medial, and final sounds in spoken one-syllable words Segments spoken words into phonemes	Reads common digraphs Decodes regular one-syllable words Knows spellings for long vowels Counts syllables in printed words Decodes two-syllable words Reads inflectional endings Decodes grade 1 irregular words Distinguishes long/short vowels Knows more vowel spelling sounds teams	Reads grade-level texts Has good expression, accuracy, and rate Uses context to self-correct word recognition
2ND GRADE			
None	None	Decodes two-syllable words/long vowels Identifies words with common but inconsistent spellings/sounds Decodes common prefixes and suffixes	Reads grade-level texts Has good expression, accuracy, and rate Uses context to self-correct word recognition

cognitive resources for comprehending and thinking with language and text. (There is more detail on this linkage in Chapter 7.)

The grade-level standards for reading foundations from the CCSS are summarized in Table 5.2. The grade-level progression for word reading included in the section labeled "phonics" is generally consistent with the research on the developmental sequence of learning to read. However, the PA standards for kindergarten focus more on phonological awareness (rhyming, syllables) than on phonemic awareness. Recall that the ability to attend to and manipulate individual phonemes (phonemic awareness) is necessary and well within the learning capability of older preschool and kindergarten children. A notable omission from the CCSS on reading foundations is a sufficient emphasis on extended opportunities to read child-selected books that are aligned with the phonics (word decoding) skills children have been taught. PreK standards are increasingly identifying alphabet knowledge and phonemic awareness ability. However, these standards often specify only very initial levels for alphabet knowledge and phonemic awareness. Knowledge of a few letter names or the ability to detect rhymes or clap syllables are examples of these initial levels. Research confirms that when preschool children, including DLLs, participate in effective instruction as identified within this chapter, many can identify beginning sounds in words and those who achieve knowledge of many letters of the alphabet may learn to decode simple words.

Educational Principles from Chapter 5

1. Establish a strong emphasis on teaching the alphabet, phonemic awareness, and word decoding from PreK through grade 2.
2. Provide teachers and their students a rich set of materials with which to teach the three essential foundations.
3. Ensure that all teaching staff have accurate knowledge of the structure of English and how this applies to alphabetic, phonemic awareness, and word decoding instruction.
4. Use similar lesson plan rubrics and materials to support learning reading foundations from PreK through grade 2.

Teaching Practices From Chapter 5

1. Teach reading foundations appropriate for children's developmental level to EBs of all levels of English proficiency.
2. Plan lessons that explicitly state the learning goal, maintain that focus, teach no more than one to two skills, provide ample practice, involve oral participation, extend lesson content to meaningful and authentic use, and support children's engagement.
3. Teach children the meaning of the words regularly used to teach the alphabet, phonemic awareness, and word reading.
4. Carefully plan the sequence of letter instruction to take into account letter difficulty and ensure that children do not confuse letters.
5. Teach the complete alphabet.
6. Model and teach children to accurately pronounce letter names and letter sounds.
7. Provide a lot of practice and repetition in pairing the letter name/sound to the letter shape.
8. Provide many opportunities for children to discriminate one letter from other letters.
9. Teach children to write the letters correctly.
10. Provide many opportunities for children to see and write letters for meaningful and real-world purposes.
11. Use oral language, rather than print, for initial development of phonemic awareness.
12. Help children stay focused on word structure during phonemic awareness instruction.
13. Make phonemes concrete by using manipulatives to represent them.
14. Make phonemes concrete by teaching the mouth movements to represent them.
15. Select one-syllable, common words of two to four phonemes for initial phonemic awareness instruction.
16. Teach the complete system of grapheme-phoneme correspondences, beginning with those that consistently link one phoneme to one grapheme.
17. Provide children with extensive opportunities to read texts that are decodable with the word reading knowledge they have.
18. Teach and assess for both accuracy and speed in all three foundational skills.
19. Respond to deficiencies in speed by determining why children are slowed and provide additional instruction and practice in the knowledge they need.
20. Provide children with extensive opportunities to read texts that are based on the word reading knowledge they have and that are interesting to them.

CHAPTER 6

Expanding Vocabulary and Concepts

Important Research Findings About Vocabulary

- The vocabulary gap between at-risk and other children has not been closed by classroom practice or within research studies.
- Children learn the vocabulary taught in vocabulary interventions, but this growth does not lead to overall vocabulary growth.
- The vocabulary learning of EBs will need to proceed at an accelerated rate to reach vocabulary knowledge commensurate with that of English fluent children.
- Explicit approaches to teach vocabulary directly are more effective than implicit approaches.
- Oral read-alouds and independent reading of narrative and informational text are two of the most effective implicit methods for vocabulary learning.
- The amount of time devoted to vocabulary instruction in classrooms needs to be increased.
- There is intensive need for comprehensive vocabulary programs specifying a PreK–2 sequence of communicative, academic, and instructional vocabulary words to be learned.

Vocabulary knowledge is a significant part of the semantic domain of English oral proficiency. Young children's vocabulary knowledge is highly predictive of later reading comprehension and conceptual learning (NICHD Early Child Care Research Network, 2005). One of the reasons that vocabulary knowledge contributes so significantly to reading comprehension is that is interrelated with other language and literacy skills. Good vocabulary helps children learn phonemic awareness and decoding. Children's exposure to written vocabulary words will support their word learning, word reading, and word spelling.

There are differences in children's English vocabulary knowledge based on family income and first language (Kieffer, 2012). These differences are evident when children first enter school, and they remain or intensify over the course of children's school experience (Cunningham & Stanovich, 1997). In fact, research suggests that schooling has done little to reduce these disparities in vocabulary knowledge.

Children learn words in a first or second language according to the same basic process they use to acquire overall language proficiency:

- Receiving high-quality vocabulary *input*
- *Intake* of the words to form memories of them, including what they mean, how they are pronounced, and how they are written (once children have alphabet knowledge)
- *Output* or use of the words in spoken and written language

The input, intake, and output process that applies for vocabulary learning is detailed in Chapter 3.

There are several ways in which educational practice can be developed to increase the vocabulary knowledge of EBs. One goal of this chapter is to create an understanding of vocabulary instruction that integrates the ideas of selecting the words to teach based on a well-reasoned developmental continuum, teaching a sufficient number of words, and teaching those words using practices that have been shown to be most effective for vocabulary growth (see Figure 6.1). Another goal is to explain the reasons why educators should have a sense of urgency with respect to EBs' need for greatly expanded intensity and quality of vocabulary instruction in order to meet their promise for language and literacy achievement.

CONSIDERING QUESTIONS ABOUT VOCABULARY INSTRUCTION

Which words should be selected for teaching?

Educational Principle 1: Acquire/develop a comprehensive word sequence for the words to be taught at each level, PreK through grade 2, that specifies words for basic communication, academic learning, and words used in instruction.

Educational Principle 2: Evaluate all curriculum materials considered for classroom use for the clarity and quality of the rationale for selection of the vocabulary words identified within it.

A program with promise for systematically and extensively increasing EBs' vocabulary knowledge will have at its foundation a conceptually based progression of words to be learned PreK–2. This vocabulary continuum would include

- Vocabulary needed for *communicative competence*, for *academic learning*, and for understanding *classroom instruction*
- Highly useful, generative words that would support learning of other related

Figure 6.1. Factors That Contribute to Vocabulary Growth

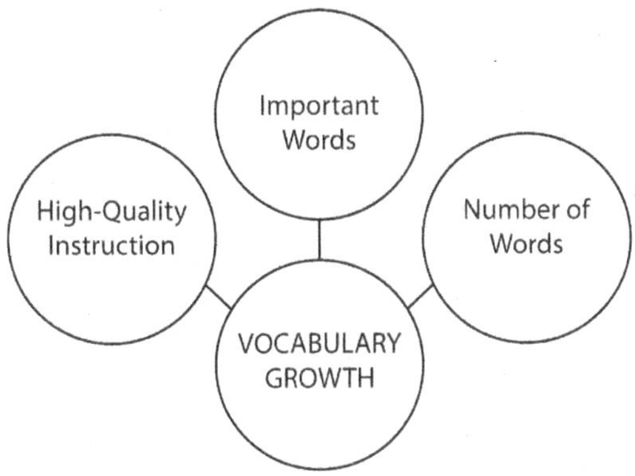

words (for example, the word *happy* would lead to the words *ecstatic*, *exhilarating*, and *joyous*)

- Core words related to subject areas (*observation*, *data*, *biology*, *organism*, *living*)
- Challenging words not easily learned from day-to-day interactions

It is important to avoid teaching together words that children might confuse. Words that look alike in print, sound the same, and are very similar or opposite in meaning should not be taught together. You may think that teaching hot and cold will help children distinguish their meanings because they are so different. Yet, you may actually find children thinking that winter is hot and summer is cold! The availability of word continuums would be second on my "wish list" of the most important educational changes needed to realize strong EB language and literacy achievement.

> ***Apply Your Knowledge:*** An ELD program for 1st-graders specifies teaching the names of colors and the words *swing, slide,* and *bicycle* to kindergarten EBs. Are these good word choices for teaching? Apply the bulleted list above as you construct your answer.

> ***Apply Your Knowledge:*** Let's evaluate the words selected for instruction within your classroom. Gather a few curricular materials (literacy, language, science, social studies, math) that you are most curious about with respect to their quality of vocabulary instruction. Identify the words that are recommended for teaching. Is a rationale given for why these words were selected? Classify the words into communicative, academic, and classroom instruction categories. What did your review tell you about the nature of words to be taught in the selected materials?

(In case you are wondering, the first item would be bilingualism as the goal for every EB.) A recent analysis of four kindergarten core reading programs found that the majority of programs had no clear basis for how words were taught or the number of words taught (Wright & Neuman, 2013).

Teaching Practice 1: Plan a vocabulary teaching program that includes words that are most useful for *basic communication, academic learning,* and *understanding instruction.*

How Many Words Need to Be Taught?

The number of words EB children will need to learn to secure a solid footing in English vocabulary knowledge is not clear, nor is it clear if their potential word learning rate is the same from year to year. Nevertheless, looking at the rate and level of vocabulary development of native English speakers may give some clues. These speakers learn 1,000–2,000 root words per year, or three to seven words per day. So, EBs would need to learn at least 1,000 basic root words (the words *help* and *helping* have the same root, for example) to stay even. The average 3-year-old English speaker knows about 1,000 root words, the average kindergartner knows about 3,000 root words, and the average 2nd-grader knows about 5,000–6,000. If children enter kindergarten as brand-new EBs, they are likely to have a 2,000–3,000-word gap. Essentially then, an EB kindergartner needs a rate of English vocabulary learning at least double what is typical for native English speakers to close the word gap.

There are estimates that children can learn about 400 words per year from instruction and that children typically learn about 40–50% of the words they are taught (Biemiller & Boote, 2006). Therefore, to learn 400 words, 1,000 would need to be taught, or about 28 words per week. How does this number compare to the number of words that you currently teach? Where might children acquire those other minimum 600 words? Implicit vocabulary learning practices where teaching word meanings is not the primary purpose can be called upon to help because implicit practices can also lead to learning vocabulary. These implicit word learning options provide important avenues for EBs to learn enough words for average yearly growth (1,000) and the vocabulary acceleration necessary. Vocabulary-enriched language occurs at a very fast clip all day long (during classroom entry and exit, on the way to or during meals, during art, in collaborative learning, on the playground, during conversations). Free choice is also an important source of implicit vocabulary learning. Other effective implicit methods include reading aloud to children, and once children can read, wide, regular, and extensive reading of narrative and informational text, particularly text they are interested in and want to read. Nothing less has a chance of being sufficient. (See Figure 6.2 for a summary of these estimates.)

Teaching Practice 2: Emphasize breadth of vocabulary learning for young EB children at beginning levels of English proficiency. Teach approximately 25-30 carefully selected new words each week.

Figure 6.2. Vocabulary Learning Numbers

- English fluent (EF) children learn 1,000–2,000 words a year.
- By age 3, EF children know about 1,000 words.
- By age 5, EF children know about 3,000 words.
- By age 7, EFs know about 5,000–7,000 words.
- Children need to be taught about 1,000 words in order to learn 400 of them from direct vocabulary instruction (about 28 words per week).
- EBs need to learn about twice as many words as EF children from kindergarten through grade 2 to close the word gap.
- More than half of the word learning rate EBs require to come abreast of EF children needs to come from sources other than direct instruction.

Teaching Practice 3: Provide rich vocabulary during every classroom activity or routine.

Teaching Practice 4: Use explicit and implicit practices to increase vocabulary knowledge.

> *Apply Your Knowledge:* Do the math on your classroom vocabulary instruction. Use the same materials that you used in the last Apply Your Knowledge exercise. Figure a way to determine about how many vocabulary words you target for instruction each week. What is 40% of that number (the number that each child is likely to learn) each week? Multiply that by 36 (the average number of weeks of school per year) to determine how many words a child might learn. How does it compare with what is shown in Figure 6.2?

How Much Does First Language Vocabulary Help EBs Learn New Vocabulary?

When EB students are learning new English vocabulary, their knowledge of the word and what it represents is activated in their first language, if the word is known. And this is a big *if*—because estimates show that about 70% of the total words young EBs know are known in one language only. The likelihood that there are similar words (cognates) to the English word in a child's L1 depends upon how similar the two languages are. Most of the logic of hopeful transfer from L1 knowledge to L2 word learning is based on comparisons of English and Spanish, which are fairly similar. There are also false cognates—words that are written or sound similarly in English and the other language but that do not actually share meaning. In dual-immersion classrooms, or when the majority of EB children and the teacher are Spanish-speaking, it is possible to provide a translation for a word or the meaning. These L1–L2 connections can help children learn the English word. But the connections do not happen automatically; teaching is needed. I believe the jury is out on whether and how potential word knowledge in L1 can be enlisted to help children, particularly young children, learn words in English.

PRINCIPLES OF HIGH-QUALITY EXPLICIT VOCABULARY INSTRUCTION

A fair amount is known about how to help children learn words. Explicit approaches to directly teach vocabulary lead to learning more words than implicit approaches in which words are embedded in an activity and not intentionally explained (Marulis & Neuman, 2013). As discussed earlier, it is important to explain the meaning of words used during instruction. There are words of instruction related to vocabulary that many EBs will not understand. To wait for children to figure them out will result in their missing out on important learning or becoming frustrated and bewildered. Important instructional words related to vocabulary learning include *word, vocabulary, sentence, definition,* and *explain.*

Teaching Practice 5: Teach the meaning of words that children will need to understand vocabulary instruction.

There is no doubt that it is a very big challenge to implement what is known into daily classroom instruction with sufficient intensity and quality to lead to the accelerated vocabulary growth EBs need. In a recent study in 55 kindergarten classrooms, Wright (2012) observed classrooms over 4 days and found almost no planned vocabulary instruction. Another study found that core reading curricula offered little support for vocabulary acceleration based on the instructional routines recommended within them (Wright & Neuman, 2013).

There are four general principles for explicit vocabulary instruction that will lead to vocabulary learning. I will discuss each in turn.

Clearly Convey the Meaning of Words and Their Labels

The first principle is that children must receive a clear understanding of the meaning of the word and connect it to its verbal label. There are several ways to accomplish this, with no clear evidence for superiority of one method over the others. Choose what you like from the menu. Practices to make sure children acquire a clear semantic (meaning-based) understanding include giving explicit, child-friendly definitions; using pictures, gestures, and demonstrations to support meaning; increasing the number and types of interactions with the new word; using the word in different contexts; and relating the word to other words and student experiences.

Provide explicit child-friendly definitions. When teachers provide a simple, clear, age-appropriate definition of a word that appears in a story or as part of a lesson, children learn the word better than when they have to figure out the meaning on their own. It is EBs who may benefit most from definitions because children with less vocabulary knowledge benefit most when teachers elaborate on words' meanings. Children's dictionaries, particularly the Collins COBUILD dictionaries (e.g., Sinclair, 2002), can help you find child-friendly definitions. Compare these examples:

> American Heritage: *predict*: To state, tell about, or make known in advance.
> COBUILD: *predict*: If you predict an event, you say that it will happen.

Teaching Practice 6: Provide explicit, child-friendly definitions.

Use pictures, gestures, and demonstrations. Gestures, objects, and pictures to explain a word will help EBs acquire its meaning. The help will be greatest when you coordinate your gesturing, pointing, or showing of a picture with your verbal labeling of it. To illustrate, touching the picture of the den right when you say it in the sentence "What is a bear *den*?" will help children connect the verbal label with the meaning. Why are the following sentences likely to help EBs learn the meaning of the target words? "Show me the picture where the boy is *smirking*." "How does your body look if you are *tense*?" "Show me how you *nod* your head." "This part of the flower is the *stem*."

Teaching Practice 7: Point to, show, or demonstrate new words.

Increase the number and types of interactions with new words. Provide ways for children to use new words multiple times. The following examples show responses of increasing difficulty for children of different English proficiency levels. Include exercises where children sometimes simply recognize the new word and at other times retrieve it from memory and say it.

- **Ask yes/no questions about the word:** "Nod your head yes or no if any of these things are a path: a bridge across a river; a highway for cars; a walking trail for people; a soccer field."
- **Ask students to complete a sentence about a word:** You provide a sentence to get started and model the structure of how to respond. "The ramp into the portable classroom helps . . ." "To make a ramp you need to . . ." "A rectangle is different from a triangle because . . ."
- **Ask open-ended questions about the word:** Once you know that children have basic knowledge of the word and concept, offer opportunities for creativity and for them to demonstrate their knowledge. "Tell your buddy what you could do in a bear den." EBs will respond to open-ended questions if they discover the enjoyment, creativity, and autonomy allowed.

Teaching Practice 8: Increase the number and types of exposures to new words.

Use the word in different contexts. After you teach a word directly, point out how it is used in a variety of sentence and story contexts: "Remember our word *ramp*?

In today's story you read about the *ramps* used for skateboarding. Where are some places in the city or other buildings where you have seen *ramps?*"

Teaching Practice 9: Use new words in different contexts.

Relate the new word to other words. After children have a firm grasp on initial meaning for a new word, exercises to connect new words to other words will integrate this new knowledge with children's existing word knowledge. When words are accurately connected to other words, there are more ways that a word can be found in memory. When the word *hook* is related to the words *catch, fish,* and *stream,* there are more clues to be used to find all of those words in memory. It is like getting your sock drawer organized. Ask children to think about words that mean the same or opposite, or are related to the vocabulary word: "What is the opposite of *less?*" "What are other words for the word *fragrant?*" "Sort these pictures into two groups: *bear, den, dog, crate, horse, barn, person, apartment building.*"

Help Children Remember a New Word and Its Meaning

The second principle is that instruction to help children *remember* the word and its meaning is necessary. Remembering a word is a two-part process: Children must cement into memory both the meaning and the word label. Thus, instruction to consolidate word meaning and word pronunciations is needed. You have probably had the experience, as have I, of knowing an idea or concept that you want to express, but you can't remember the right word. Similarly, crossword puzzles provide meanings for which the puzzle-worker must retrieve the word from memory. On the other hand, you might hear a word such as *feral,* recognize that you have heard it before, and have a vague idea that it has something to do with cats in your town. But you can't really pin down exactly what it means. Strong word memories permit children to use words for understanding and expressing meaning in oral and written language. Repetition; providing a repeated, clear, and accurate pronunciation that children also speak; having children practice decoding a word; and regularly reviewing and connecting new words to children's existing word knowledge will help children embed new meanings and the associated word labels into memory.

Teaching Practice 10: Review the meaning of vocabulary words taught in explicit instruction and read-alouds.

Repeat the new word. Repetition of meanings helps us remember words just as repetition of a phone number helps us remember it. Repetition seems to be most effective when review is spaced, with time between repetitions—but not too much time. Children may need as many as 16–24 repetitions to remember a new vocabulary word.

Make sure that both teacher and children pronounce the word correctly. Oral pronunciation will help PreK–2 EBs connect words to their meanings. For grade 1 and grade 2 children, hearing the word while they see its printed form will help them quickly connect the word to its meaning when they encounter it in text. When teachers mispronounce vocabulary, children's understanding will be hindered when they hear it spoken accurately. Children are also at increased risk of not being understood if they repeat a teacher's mispronunciation.

Teaching Practice 11: Repeat new words.

Practice decoding/reading the word. K–2 vocabulary instruction that coordinates the word meaning with decoding or reading the word helps children remember the word and its meaning. It also helps children read the word when they encounter it in text and increases the likelihood that they will use it in writing (Rosenthal & Ehri, 2007; Vadasy & Sanders, 2015). Even brief exposure to the printed word, noticing the word spelling, seems to help students learn the word meaning when they know a moderate number of alphabet letters. Showing printed words to preschool EBs who know alphabet letters can be expected to help them remember word meaning. This type of exposure should be quick and integrated with teaching word meaning.

Teaching Practice 12: Make sure that both teacher and children pronounce new words correctly.

Teaching Practice 13: Show the printed form of new words.

Teaching Practice 14: Practice decoding/reading new words.

Review meanings of new words. Review taught vocabulary words over the course of days, weeks, and months. Review might be done in a brief mini-lesson where children are reminded, "Let's review all the words you learned about plant growth." Pictures for each word and the child-friendly definition used to introduce it can be reviewed one after the other. Less explicit but perhaps less efficient review may include the following: briefly reminding students of word meanings, helping children use the word during class discussions, giving additional examples of the word in different sentence contexts, and showing the printed word as the meaning is reviewed. Research suggests that when words are first taught they should be reviewed frequently, perhaps daily. Subsequent reviews can be spaced further apart.

Support, Encourage, and Inspire Children to Use New Words

The third principle of high-quality vocabulary instruction is that it supports, encourages, and inspires children to comprehend and use the words they learn in both oral and written language. This is the penultimate way that new vocabulary becomes deeply, completely, and personally integrated into children's language system. I believe this is one feature of vocabulary instruction that is rarely included in practice. This feature is particularly appropriate for young EBs in teaching communicative

> *Apply Your Knowledge:* In this exercise you will continue evaluating the materials you selected for the two previous exercises (nature and number of vocabulary words identified). This time, you will find evidence on the quality of the vocabulary instruction practices recommended in the materials. Review the instructional routines based on Teaching Principles 5–8. What conclusions about vocabulary instruction are supported by what you found?

language vocabulary where opportunity to use newly learned words may occur more frequently than does opportunity to use academic vocabulary.

Academic vocabulary for young children whose social studies and science content often connects to their daily lives may also be more readily used than academic language for older children.

For example, imagine children are learning about plant growth and the vocabulary words *photosynthesis, stem, trunk, chlorophyll,* and *plant.* The class goes for a walk during which the students are asked to use the new words whenever they see something that applies. Oral reading and discussion of informational text is useful for creating contexts that call forth newly learned academic words that are unlikely to occur spontaneously. A read-aloud of an informational book on plants would be ideal.

Teachers will need to think carefully about how they can increase children's oral and written use of new vocabulary. Pause for a moment to consider this challenge. Examples taken from a PreK classroom include:

- Posting the word *look* or a picture of someone *looking* on a word wall with other new words
- Having children place a mark on a 3 x 5 card under each word each time it is used throughout the day(s)
- Grouping words together for use in an activity

For example, after the walk, children might take turns telling their buddy about the plant words they encountered on the walk.

Teaching Practice 15: Develop spoken and written activities in which children will encounter and use new vocabulary words.

Help Children Deepen and Extend the Meanings of Words

The final principle of high-quality vocabulary instruction is to deepen and extend initial meanings that have become firmly rooted. For example, the word *look* as in "look at me" is explicitly taught. The teacher enacts the high-quality instructional practices: child-friendly definition, use in a sentence, demonstration, pronunciation, practice, repetition, spelling, and affirmation that children understand the word based on their response when the teacher says, "Look at me" or "Look at the playhouse." The teacher extends this basic understanding to help children know what it means to "look" for evidence. He or she might have children hide something and then proceed to look in several places, saying "look" as they search each location. This lesson extends and deepens initial understanding consistent with what is meant in the CCSS by the terms *nuance* and *shades of meaning*.

The value of depth of word learning compared to breadth of word learning for PreK–2 EBs isn't known. However, the great word gap between EB and English fluent children *is* known. Therefore, breadth of word learning seems logically to merit greater attention for children who are novice learners of English and have a great need for acquiring both communicative and academic language. Multiple exposures and opportunities to actively process word meanings are especially important for learning academic and content vocabulary. These words must be learned more deeply for productive use in student speaking and writing. I suggest consulting the Text Project website (http://www.textproject.org/classroom-materials/vocabulary/e4/) for free vocabulary lessons and materials incorporating practices for both depth and breadth of word learning.

Teaching Practice 16: After a word is known well, extend and deepen word meaning, particularly for content areas such as math, arts, science, and so on.

ENCOURAGING INCIDENTAL AND INDEPENDENT VOCABULARY LEARNING

It isn't possible to directly teach enough vocabulary to ensure that EBs acquire the number of new words they need for strong academic achievement. Fortunately, vocabulary learning occurs during conversations and discussion with teachers who use varied language (see Chapter 3), when children are read texts with challenging and many vocabulary words, and during independent reading. (See Figure 6.3 for how to involve families in helping their EB children expand their vocabulary.) Oral language experiences exposing EBs to new words and engaging them in conversations about texts that feature sophisticated vocabulary, varied sentence structures, and academic vocabulary are recommended.

Reading Aloud to Children

Reading books aloud probably has more research support for its potential to build children's vocabulary—particularly children who are not yet readers—than any other practice. It occurs as often as two to three times a day—every day—in high-quality preschool programs. The frequency at which adults read aloud to children decreases from kindergarten to grade 2.

But not all read-alouds are created equal. A particularly important practice for promoting vocabulary learning is the teacher's direct attention to explaining im-

Figure 6.3. How to Involve Families in Helping Their Emergent Bilingual Children Expand Their Vocabulary and Concepts

- Acquire a basic picture dictionary for all children. Have children take these dictionaries home on a regular basis.
- In English, label, tell about, and show the pictures of English vocabulary items they are learning.
- Encourage families to use unusual, long and challenging words when talking to children.
- Encourage families to use more than one word for the same thing.
- Encourage families to regularly set aside time for children to pretend read and read books (in either L1 or English) they choose and find interesting.
- Help families access books for at-home reading.

portant and interesting words. The previous practices detailed in the section titled Principles of High-Quality Explicit Vocabulary Instruction apply. There are a few new vocabulary learning practices that march hand in hand with read-alouds. One of these practices is to read stories several times. Repeated readings—up to three to four times—are associated with increasing word learning with each reading. However, stories need to be interesting or else this kind of repeated reading can become disengaging for children. A second feature of the most effective read-alouds is that teachers and children share interactive talk during them. Teachers should respond, elaborate on, and ask questions that mirror the interactive principles described within the ERECT Language model discussed in Chapter 3 (refer to Figure 3.8). Read-alouds of both narrative and informational text add to children's vocabulary. Narratives are more likely to support communicative vocabulary learning and informational texts to support academic, content-related vocabulary. Increasing the number of opportunities that EBs have to listen to great stories and learn about the physical and social world through read-alouds is strongly recommended. Read-alouds and independent book reading are similar in that they both involve learning words while interacting with connected, meaningful language. EBs will benefit from having much more of both.

Teaching Practice 17: Read a book aloud and read it aloud again, accompanying reading with interactive talk and explanation of key vocabulary words.

Independent Reading of Narrative and Informational Text

As children's word reading skill grows, simply reading becomes a significant way for them to learn new vocabulary. Even 20 minutes of daily reading is estimated to result in learning 1,000 new words each year for students who can decode and comprehend well (Nagy, Anderson, & Herman, 1985). Therefore, independent reading is potentially a huge boost to EBs' vocabulary learning. Revisit Figure 6.2 for a reminder of how significant learning 1,000 words a year is.

Teaching Practice 18: Provide children with a minimum of 15 minutes a day to read self-selected books that have rich vocabulary.

Students are more likely to acquire new vocabulary through independent reading if they have strong word reading skills, and if they read books that are well matched to their reading level and rich in vocabulary. The importance of reading text as a source of higher-level vocabulary is illustrated in research showing that students encounter 50% more rare words (those not likely to be in the typical student's vocabulary) in children's books than in television or adult conversations. Further, print information provides a richness and literary quality that is lacking in many electronic information sources or personal experiences.

Apply Your Knowledge: Select the word *look, see,* or *walk.* Identify other related words for kindergarten, 1st grade, and 2nd grade for which these words are an anchor. You are on your way to developing a vocabulary continuum! Go ahead and choose another word.

THE PREK–GRADE 2 CONTINUUM: EXPANDING VOCABULARY

There is an intense need to develop vocabulary PreK–2 continuums that identify the words to be taught at each level. Alternatively, and perhaps even better, would be to align these vocabulary list continuums with levels of English proficiency. These continuums should reflect that EBs have a greater need for developing communicative English compared to English fluent children by including a strand of communicative words to be taught. Recall that communicative language means the language used to manage your day with respect to relationships, activities, needs, and daily life. The words that may be most important for communicative language should be selected with the thought in mind for how they form a foundation that can be used to anchor related but rarer and more sophisticated words. For example, teaching the word *help* in preschool could become an anchor used in learning the words *assist* and *assistant* in kindergarten, and *aid*, *support,* and *benefit* in grade 1.

In 1930, Charles Ogden published a teaching program called Basic English (see Figure 6.4). It could serve as a worthy beginning for developing a PreK–2 vocabulary continuum. Figure 6.4 shows some math for how a vocabulary program for PreK– 2 creating a vocabulary continuum that included this basic vocabulary might play out. The math shows that it would be very feasible. One of many websites where you can obtain the 850 words identified by Ogden is called Basic English Words (ogden.basic-english.org/booksum1.html).

Figure 6.4. Charles Ogden's Basic English Teaching Program

- Ogden reduced the 25,000-word Oxford dictionary into 850 basic words.
- Simple line drawings with words arranged in categories were used to teach students the meaning of each word.
- If these words were distributed over the 4-year period from preschool through 2nd grade for vocabulary instruction : 850/4 = 212 words taught each year.
- 400 (estimated number of words children can learn from explicit instruction)
- 212 (Basic words to teach each year)
- 178 (words left over for academic and instructional vocabulary)

CONNECTIONS TO THE COMMON CORE STATE STANDARDS AND PRESCHOOL LEARNING STANDARDS

In this chapter, the importance of selecting which words to teach has been emphasized. Within the K–2 Common Core State Standards, word learning processes and developing relationships among words are emphasized. For example, kindergarten vocabulary standards stipulate that children should know nuance and shades of meaning. In grade 2, children are expected to use sentence context to infer meaning and to use dictionaries and glossaries. The emphasis on nuance and shades of meaning suggests that depth of vocabulary knowledge is more important than breadth. For EBs who have so many words to learn, breadth of vocabulary learning may actually be more important. Furthermore, the standards within the CCSS do not recognize the different types of vocabulary knowledge that are equally important for young EBs who are learning the basics of English communication, academic vocabulary, and the words used during instruction. PreK learning standards are even less specific about what vocabulary preschoolers should know. Head Start standards for both receptive and expressive language stipulate that children should know and use increasingly complex and varied vocabulary.

Educational Principles From Chapter 6

1. Acquire/develop a comprehensive word sequence for the words to be taught at each level, PreK through grade 2, that specifies words for basic communication, academic learning, and words used in instruction.
2. Evaluate all curriculum materials considered for classroom use for the clarity and quality of the rationale for selection of the vocabulary words identified within it.

Teaching Practices from Chapter 6

1. Plan a vocabulary teaching program that includes words that are most useful for basic communication, academic learning, and understanding instruction.
2. Emphasize breadth of vocabulary learning for young EB children at beginning levels of English proficiency. Teach approximately 25-30 carefully selected new words each week.
3. Provide rich vocabulary during every classroom activity or routine.
4. Use explicit and implicit practices to increase vocabulary knowledge.
5. Teach the meaning of words that children will need to understand vocabulary instruction.
6. Provide explicit, child-friendly definitions.
7. Point to, show, or demonstrate new words.
8. Increase the number and types of exposures to new words.
9. Use new words in different contexts.
10. Review the meaning of vocabulary words taught in explicit instruction and read-alouds.
11. Repeat new words.
12. Make sure that both teacher and children pronounce new words correctly.
13. Show the printed form of new words.
14. Practice decoding/reading new words.
15. Develop spoken and written activities in which children will encounter and use new vocabulary words.
16. After a word is known well, extend and deepen word meaning, particularly for content areas such as math, arts, science, and so on.
17. Read a book aloud and read it aloud again, accompanying reading with interactive talk and explanation of key vocabulary words.
18. Provide children with 15 minutes a day to read self-selected books that have rich vocabulary.

CHAPTER 7

Advancing Comprehending and Thinking with Text and Language

Important Research Findings About Comprehending and Thinking with Text and Language

- Listening comprehension and reading comprehension are highly correlated.
- Children with limited English oral proficiency can perform high-level thinking about text.
- Fast and accurate word reading frees mental resources for comprehension and thinking.
- Good comprehension and thinking about text depends on ongoing teacher instruction.
- There is limited evidence on effective teaching practices for enhancing comprehension in K–2 children.
- Oral and written retelling is an effective practice for promoting and monitoring comprehension.
- Visualization of text and oral discourse meanings is an effective practice for promoting and monitoring comprehension.
- Children need to develop awareness of their own comprehension and thinking and to apply actions and strategies to monitor and improve it.
- Instructional language used to talk about comprehending and thinking is very challenging for EBs.
- An accurate text representation is an essential foundation for advanced thinking.
- Activating children's first language can leverage their higher-order thinking.

Oral comprehension and thinking with language are intertwined with a host of language competencies for both EBs and English fluent children. Children who can read words quickly and accurately, know the meaning of many words, know how English is structured, and are able to integrate all of these competencies for discourse-level

Figure 7.1. Major Components of Emergent Bilinguals' Oral and Text Comprehension

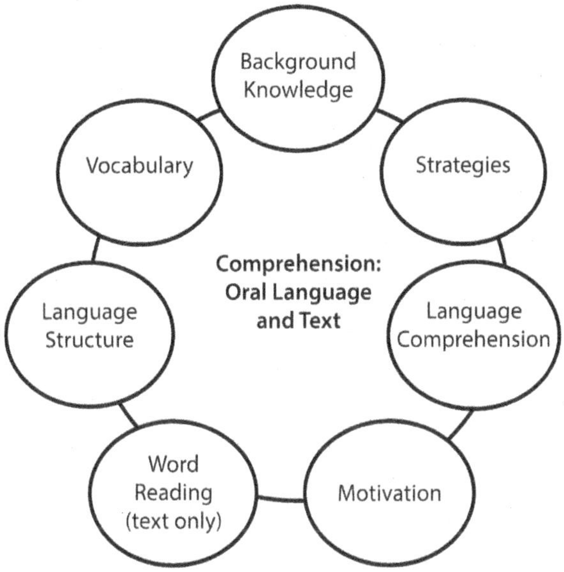

understanding will be poised for good comprehension and reasoning. Accurately connecting text meaning with background knowledge can aid comprehension and reasoning. The ability and inclination to apply strategies for comprehending and thinking and to self-monitor "online" understanding while listening and reading are additional important competencies. Figure 7.1 provides an illustration of the seven major components of oral and text comprehension.

An effective instructional program for EBs will include all these components in an integrated system where each component is valued by teachers and afforded careful curriculum planning, high-quality instruction, and well-designed learning activities. In Chapters 4, 5, and 6, I have addressed the important components of language structure, word reading, and vocabulary. You can see from Figure 7.1 that understanding EB children's development and mastering the instructional practices for these three topics will promote comprehending and thinking with language and text. In this chapter, I will focus more on thinking processes and the features of oral or written discourse that influence comprehending and thinking. Throughout the chapter, I will use the term *discourse* extensively because it captures both oral and written language and keeps at the forefront the idea that it is understanding of integrated and extended blocks of language that is at the heart of comprehending and thinking with language and text.

Teaching Practice 1: Provide instruction in language structure, word reading efficiency, vocabulary, and language comprehension strategies to support comprehension and thinking lessons.

Apply Your Knowledge: Analyze your comprehension teaching program by making a list of the practices you regularly use to teach each of seven major influences on oral and reading comprehension shown in Figure 7.1.

MAXIMIZING MENTAL RESOURCES FOR COMPREHENSION AND THINKING

The human mental system has a limited capacity. It can only think about and process a certain amount of information. EBs are likely to have an increased demand on their cognitive resources while comprehending and thinking with text and language because of their limited English proficiency. I am sure as adults we have all had the experience of "I can't think about one more thing." To some degree, this is an expression of the limited capacity of the human mental system. Therefore, an important way to support the comprehension and thinking efficiency of children who are learning English is to free up as many mental resources as possible for this demanding mental work.

One of the most significant ways that mental comprehending and thinking resources can be maximized for literacy achievement is through word reading efficiency. When children have high levels of word reading speed and accuracy—word reading efficiency—they do not have to devote as much of their limited thinking capacity to word reading. If 2nd-grade student Yarizel has difficulty accessing the meaning of the words *dog* and *ecstatic* in the sentence "The dog is ecstatic" because she cannot decode the words efficiently, she will not be able to comprehend the sentence at a basic level or apply higher-order thinking to the question "Why is the dog ecstatic?"

Many EBs have limitations in word decoding (Nassaji, 2014). Word reading efficiency is not a lower-level skill whose instruction shows a lack of concern for attention to comprehension. Word reading efficiency is the key for opening the door to the wide world of ideas, concepts, artistic expression, content-area learning, and experience beyond one's own that is available in text. High levels of competence with vocabulary, language structure, and comprehension strategy application will also help EB children have more mental resources for comprehension and thinking.

Teaching Practice 2: Increase children's word reading efficiency.

HOW TO BUILD COMPREHENSION

The Relationship Between Listening Comprehension and Reading Comprehension

Reading comprehension and listening comprehension are highly related. One influential model of reading called the Simple View of Reading (Hoover & Gough, 1990) states that reading competence can be well explained as a combination of listening comprehension and word reading efficiency. This relationship means that building PreK–2 listening comprehension can support later text comprehension. Listening comprehension can develop during a storybook read-aloud when an adult is typically doing most of the talking. Listening and understanding discourse is required in conversation with teachers and peers, finding solutions to problems expressed by children about classroom life, and language-infused cooperative play. Research shows that children's oral narrative ability—the ability to tell a story, explain a series of events, or recount personal experiences—is a powerful predictor of reading comprehension.

The importance of oral comprehension also implies that for EBs with limited English proficiency, listening to discourse (stories and informational hunks of language integrated together) can be an effective practice for fostering text comprehension. This is a very powerful idea that constrains to some degree the extensive talk about the necessity of reading complex text. Using listening comprehension is a means of responding to teachers' sharp awareness and concern that these texts may be overwhelming for EBs. So let's have a big shout-out—literally—for oral comprehension exercises.

Teaching Practice 3: Provide many listening comprehension activities with narrative and informational discourse.

Balancing Text Knowledge with Background Knowledge

Reading comprehension has long been recognized as an interaction between reader characteristics and the characteristics and meanings within text (van den Broek & Espin, 2012). Practices to activate and draw upon children's background knowledge (BK) have been a treasured staple of comprehension instruction for at least 20 years. Questions to activate background knowledge may be used before, during, or after listening to or reading discourse. This practice has been particularly valued by teachers sensitive to EBs because it recognizes and draws upon their unique experiences, which may differ from those of mainstream learners. The growing focus on (1) text or discourse comprehension and (2) informational text is shifting attention away from children's personal background knowledge toward attention on the information and meaning within the oral or written discourse. Children may learn to show "right there" in the text or point to a part of a picture where they have found evidence for answering a question or explaining a main idea. Thus, there is increasing emphasis on growing rather than activating background knowledge.

I believe this recalibration is needed. Inaccurate, idiosyncratic, tangential, and incomplete learning can occur when any and all background knowledge is treated as beneficial. Many of you may have experienced valiantly trying to incorporate comments from students into lesson objectives, even though, try as you might, you could not see the connection. Helping EBs comprehend oral and written discourse through instruction that builds or draws upon children's *relevant* and *accurate* background knowledge is valuable. I recommend the following practices:

- Assess the likelihood that children have relevant background knowledge.
- When children are likely to have limited BK, pre-teach information that is related to the discourse (vocabulary, concepts).
- Develop BK using nonverbal materials (graphics, pictures, video, demonstration).
- Teach children to rely on BK that "goes with" the oral or written discourse (use guiding questions and request children to show the connection verbally, with pictures, or through demonstration).
- Quickly and succinctly tie the BK children provide/share to the oral or written discourse.
- Activate student BK/experience *after* oral or written presentation of the material to be learned.

The contribution that relevant background knowledge can add to comprehending and thinking with language and text is a reminder that should be taken to heart about the importance of science, the arts, social studies, math, and other areas of knowledge. This breadth may be especially important for EBs from low-income families where resources for developing extensive background knowledge are likely to be limited.

Teaching Practice 4: Provide a comprehensive curriculum that includes significant learning about science, the arts, social studies, and math.

Teaching Practice 5: Use practices that ensure relevant background knowledge is developed or activated.

Teaching Practice 6: Keep the relationship of background knowledge to the oral or written discourse in focus during lessons.

Strategies for Comprehending and Thinking with Language and Text

A strategy is a deliberate and purposeful method or plan, which for our discussion refers to ways, often mental, to improve comprehending and thinking with language and text. When preschooler Evaeh makes mental images of what is being read, summarizes, or retells at the end of each page or after a portion of oral discussion, she is using a strategy. For many if not most PreK–2 children, including EBs, these strategies must be taught, supported by teachers during their use, and eventually supported by self-activated prompts. Effective strategy use requires being taught what the strategy is and participating in learning activities where the strategy is purposefully elicited and activated. The end goal is for a child to confidently and appropriately activate the strategy and to expend the effort to use it effectively.

Many strategies have been broadly endorsed for improving reading comprehension. A review examining the extent of research support for these practices reported limited evidence for many of them, particularly for younger children (Shanahan,

Callison, Carriere, Duke, Pearson, Schatschneider, & Torgesen, 2010). Lamentably, there was no discussion specific to young EBs. Two of the strategies that were more strongly supported by the research are consistent with practices that help EBs and are appropriate for young children. Lucky day! These two strategies are *visualizing* and *retelling/summarizing*. Table 7.1 explains and gives examples of these two strategies.

Teaching Practice 7: Teach EBs to visualize, retell, and summarize oral and written discourse and to utilize these strategies during reading.

A third strategy in Table 7.1 supported by the research for EF children is called *self-monitoring*. This strategy will be much more challenging for EBs to master because it requires an understanding of the instructional language used to teach it (discussed further below). Many programs recommend using teacher modeling and think-alouds for teaching comprehension monitoring. For example, a preschool teacher reads the sentence "The dog was flying high above the houses." She performs a think-aloud to model and teach comprehension monitoring by saying, "Hmm, that is very odd; dogs don't fly. How is that happening?" Salena, a novice 4-year-old English learner, will not be helped much to get the idea of comprehension monitoring because she is investing serious effort just to see that dog flying above the houses. It may even be possible that the teacher's think-aloud is just an interruption and distraction that detracts from Salena's fragile grasp on the basic meaning of the sentence! It is encouraging that there is evidence that comprehension monitoring can be taught to preschoolers, although EBs did not participate in the study (Bianco et al., 2010).

> *Apply Your Knowledge:* The goal of self-monitoring strategy use is for children to detect when they don't understand and to correct their misunderstanding. Review the Example Activities to Teach self-monitoring in Table 7.1. The main challenge for EBs is likely to be understanding the meaning of *confused* or *unable to understand.* Can you think of two additional ways to teach these concepts to the EBs in your classroom?

Teaching Practice 8: Teach EBs to monitor comprehension with carefully designed instruction that makes the abstraction of the concept of monitoring and language to teach it more concrete.

Begin strategy instruction by establishing a basic understanding of the oral or written discourse (storybook, informational book, digital). This basic understanding will address the questions of who (if applicable), what, where, when, and why for narrative text. One engaging and effective collaborative practice for establishing a

Table 7.1. Comprehension Strategies for Emergent Bilinguals

Strategy	What It Is	Example Activities to Teach
Visualizing	Students make a mental image of what is represented in oral discourse or text.	• Explain that visualizing shows in your head what is in the text; it will help comprehension. • Place objects and pictures in front of the group. Ask students to visualize (tap head, close eyes, show thinking). • Read or state a sentence that can be easily visualized —tell what you visualize and have students practice visualizing with other sentences from oral or written discourse.
Retelling/ summarizing	Students draw, show with props, or retell a story, historical event, or scientific sequence, or provide the main ideas presented in oral discourse or text.	• Children put a set of pictures from a story on flannel boards in order. • Children are given props or pictures that show the sequence of *metamorphosis* from a text or oral discourse. • Children "tell the story" on a sheet with three boxes of diminishing sizes and write only one to two sentences in the last box. They share with a partner what they have depicted (pictures or writing) in the last box.
Self-monitoring	Children notice when they are confused or unable to understand the discourse.	• Children discuss what doesn't make sense and reorder an out-of-order set of pictures or short texts that misrepresent the sequence of taking a bath. • Children listen to or read a mixed-up story and talk about what doesn't make sense. • Provide children with a card that shows a puzzled face. Teach them to show it during oral discourse or text reading when they don't understand.

basic understanding of a discourse is to use a die with several sides labeled with these terms. Children roll the die and answer the question that comes up. Another practice is to label small cards with these terms, place them on a table, and have a child select a card and then tell who, when, what, and so on. It is fine to have more than one child answer each "W." In fact, multiple responders may scaffold for those with lower levels of English proficiency. The choice provided in the labeled cards activity is also beneficial for motivation.

Teaching Practice 9: Build a basic understanding of the oral or written discourse (story or informational text) prior to strategy application.

The practices in a study that effectively taught comprehension strategies to kindergarten EBs are shown in Figure 7.2 (Solari & Gerber, 2008). The Institute of Education Sciences (http://ies.ed.gov/ncee/wwc/practiceguide.aspx?sid=14), a federal agency supporting research and practice in education, has a number of videos,

Figure 7.2. Effective Practices for Increasing EBs' Text Comprehension

Strategies that were taught:

- Summarization of text
- Identifying the main idea in text
- Factual recall
- Prediction making
- Inference

Instructional sequence:

- Students began instruction with easier elements of comprehension (direct recall and summarization), followed by more difficult comprehension subcomponents (making predictions and inferences)

Instructional activities:

- Teachers provided guiding questions to lead students to the main idea of the passage, and to help students retain passage sequencing and facts
- Teachers introduced difficult vocabulary words through picture cards
- Teachers taught sequencing of passage events with picture sequencing with subsequent oral retell of passages

practice guides, and a research review on comprehension. I recommend that you consult these sources for additional real live lessons.

A Key to the Castle: Knowing the Language of Comprehending and Thinking

As explained above, the evidence is convincing that strategy instruction is useful and perhaps essential to support children's success when engaging with complex, challenging text and oral discourse and high-level thinking. Yet, important difficulties with this instruction for young EBs should be kept in mind. The first difficulty is that instruction about strategies refers to amorphous and abstract mental processes such as "thinking," "understanding," and "repairing." The thinking processes most frequently specified in the K–2 CCSS are *compare, evidence, retell, describe, reasons, same,* and *different.* Other concepts that frequently appear with comprehension activities include *predict, think, analyze, observe,* and *because.* Pause here for a moment to think how you could teach these words using demonstrations, acting out, visual/graphic information, or short verbal explanations. You probably found thinking of ways to teach these words at least a little bit challenging. A good rule of thumb is that when it is more difficult for you to teach something, that something is even more difficult for children to learn. These vocabulary words will be very challenging for young EBs to understand. But they will need to understand these words in order to benefit from instruction that uses them.

Teaching Practice 10: Teach children the vocabulary for and processes of comparing, retelling, describing, giving reasons, summarizing, and finding evidence.

Apply Your Knowledge: Examine the program and materials you use to teach comprehending and thinking with language and text:

» Identify the key words that children will need to be taught.
» List the comprehension strategies that are included. How do they compare with those recommended for EBs in Table 7.1 and Figure 7.2?

Leveraging First Language Strength for High-Level Comprehending and Thinking

EB children have the capacity to use high-level thinking to the same level as their English-proficient counterparts. However, they will be constrained, commensurate with their level of English proficiency, in their engagement and demonstration of this thinking in English. When EBs use their L1 for thinking and comprehending, they are afforded an opportunity to sidestep their English proficiency challenges and forge onward and upward toward the upper levels of their capabilities. Therefore, when the goal of lessons is to exercise high-level thinking, activating L1 is particularly useful. After children have had an opportunity to draw on their first language strength for thinking and reasoning, they will be better prepared and will have an invaluable foundation for making the same effort in English. Collaborative activities involving high-level thinking and deeper comprehension with others who speak the same L1 can be very effective for this purpose. Other specific suggestions for how you might activate L1 are included in Chapter 2 and in Figure 7.3.

Teaching Practice 11: Activate children's L1 for initial high-level thinking and comprehending exercises.

TEXT FOR EMERGENT BILINGUAL READERS

A Critical Look at Text Complexity

Educational Principle 1: Inform others at grade-level meetings and your site administrators about the potential difficulties for EBs associated with text complexity at grades K–2.

PreK–2 children are just beginning what all educators hope will be a long adventure with text. The first major task that beginners will encounter as they start this journey

Figure 7.3. How to Engage Families in Advancing Their Emergent Bilingual Children's Comprehension and Thinking with Language and Text

- Help families understand the 5 Ws—who, what, where, when, and why—and ask their children these questions about TV shows, movies, apps, and family and community events.
- Regularly send home a few high-level questions (translated into the first language) that parents could discuss with their children about texts, stories, or units of study from the classroom.
- Let families know about the nature and value of informational books.

is to learn the relationship of speech and print, leading to the ability to decode print and convert it into meaningful words. As explained in Chapter 5, this is a complex and difficult task that requires significant mental resources from the mental system with its limited capacity.

If texts are too difficult or do not supply the right kind of reading opportunities to speed along word reading growth, readers will become so bogged down with decoding that there will be little capacity available for comprehension. In addition, if the vocabulary and syntax of the text are too advanced, either conceptually or linguistically, the capacity system will be overwhelmed, particularly for beginners who have to exert more effort toward decoding than more advanced readers.

There is reason to be concerned about the text complexity targets that begin at grade 2 within the CCSS (Hiebert & Mesmer, 2013). These texts are likely to be far beyond the reading level of typical grade 2 children and certainly beyond the reading ability of many EBs. The Lexile level at the higher end of the text complexity band for grade 2 children designates a complexity level similar to that for grade 4 children on the National Assessment of Educational Progress (NAEP) assessment test. In the 2015 NAEP assessment, two-thirds of 4th graders were not proficient with text at this level. Furthermore, historical evidence provides no basis for concluding that primary-grade text has experienced a "dumbing down" over the past 40 years, although there is evidence of such a trend for high school text. Thus, we have a situation in which (1) there are reasonable grounds for worrying about potential unintended negative consequences, and (2) there is no recent research that primary-grade texts have decreased in difficulty or that increasing the complexity of primary-grade texts will lead to better reading competence. Texts that are too difficult to decode or understand will impede meaningful comprehending and thinking opportunity. They are also a threat to EBs' engagement, perseverance, and challenge seeking. A cautionary stance is needed.

My overall recommendation, given the heightened vulnerability of EBs to texts that are too difficult, is to provide complexity "work-arounds" via the following four instructional guidelines:

1. Pay great attention to the complexity of texts and, when possible, err on the side of selecting simpler text.

2. Include a great deal of support in the form of vocabulary instruction, unpacking of challenging sentences, and building text-related conceptual background.
3. Consider oral reading of text, particularly for a "first reading," or when more comprehending and thinking about text is the goal of instruction.
4. Make sure that complex text is balanced with less complex text, text comprised largely of words children can decode, and engaging and interesting text that children will want to read.

A final reminder is that EBs will need more language and motivation support as text complexity increases. Table 7.2 shows a number of the features of texts, related to text complexity, that will render them easier or more difficult for EBs.

Teaching Practice 12: Evaluate and select text for the level of complexity appropriate for the learning goal of every lesson.

> ***Apply Your Knowledge:*** Stand in front of a mirror. Using this section of text as a scaffold to refer to, explain the potential issues with text complexity for young EB children. Now make a bulleted list of those points and share them at a grade-level meeting, professional development session, or with site administrators.

Narrative and Informational Text

PreK–2 children have historically experienced narrative text far more than they have experienced informational text. Narrative text basically tells a story. Informational text basically communicates knowledge about topics and subjects. *The Travels of Babar* (deBrunhoff, 1932) is a narrative text, while a text describing frog development is an informational or expository text. As a reminder, both types of text are discourse. To be sure, children may learn information about rabbits from listening to the narrative text *The Runaway Bunny* (Brown, 1942). They will learn far more about rabbits from an informational book titled, say, *Rabbits: A Member of the Rodent Family.*

There is growing evidence that informational text can strengthen language and deepen and broaden the concepts and ideas that children know about. In addition, learning about the features of science, social studies, and historical texts and how to obtain meaning from them will support reading comprehension, close reading of text, and thinking with text. A recent study showed that at-risk 2nd-graders could be taught text structures within a social studies unit on historical communities. The instruction benefitted text comprehension and did not interfere with social studies learning (Williams et al., 2016). Short oral discourses of two to three sentences rather than complete books will help make the structures more obvious, particularly

Table 7.2. Features of Oral or Written Texts That Influence Text Complexity

Feature	Easier	Harder
Discourse structure	Well structured	Shifting, unclear structure
Vocabulary	Common, simple, shorter words	Uncommon, technical, longer words
Relevant background knowledge	Extensive vocabulary taught, video viewed, discussion of objectives	Limited background knowledge
Sentence/syntax	Short subject–predicate: The boy hoped to find a magic wand.	Longer, more embedding, and indirect: To find a magic wand was the hope of the boy.
Text/discourse type	Narrative	Expository
Discourse length	One sentence	Multiple sentences, complete discourse (oral, text)

Figure 7.4. Structures of Informational Text

Sequence	Comparison	Causation	Description	Problem–Solution
First Rigby ate the cheese. Then she made a nest. Finally, she went to sleep.	Rigby is a mouse. She is smaller than Tabitha. Rigby is gray while Tabitha is brown.	The cheese that Rigby ate made her sick. Her upset stomach led to her wanting to rest.	Rigby was a small dove-colored mouse. She was a very active mouse. She also loved cheese.	Rigby had an upset stomach. What could she do for her stomach? She decided to rest to calm her stomach.

for preschool and kindergarten children. Figure 7.4 shows the five most frequent structures of informational text.

Teaching Practice 13: Teach children to identify the five most common informational text structures: sequence, comparison, causation, description, and problem-solution.

Teaching Practice 14: Provide children access (oral, written, digital) to the concepts, ideas, knowledge, experiences, and people within both narrative and informational discourse.

The lack of ability to manage the diversity of text structures that occur in informational text is a major reason students often find informational text difficult. Texts about subjects such as science and social studies are also more likely to rely

Apply Your Knowledge: Here is an example of a short text constructed to illustrate several ways of signaling a sequence:

First the king raised taxes.
After the king raised taxes, the citizens revolted.
Then, soldiers were sent to stop and jail the troublemakers.
As a result of these events, a war between the king and the colonists started.
It was called the American War of Independence.

What are the words that signify a sequence? What are words that could be substituted for these? How could you rewrite the text to make it more challenging for children with more English?

upon academic language than is narrative text. Academic language is particularly demanding for preschool–grade 2 EBs because of their emerging English proficiency. Texts with demanding academic language are more likely to have:

- specialized and rarer vocabulary (*gigantic* versus *big*);
- presentation of facts, ideas, and concepts beyond students' immediate experience (an informational text on volcanoes);
- more complex and longer sentences; and
- organization that is less obvious and less like everyday talk.

Interestingly, preschool teachers' language has richer vocabulary and more complex sentences when they are discussing informational books. This is another mechanism by which informational text may support comprehension and thinking with language. Finally, children, including those of preschool age, enjoy and want to learn about the facts, concepts, and people that inhabit high-quality informational text. Introduce them regularly.

Teaching Practice 15: Read or have children read a complex text or text selection more than once.

Apply Your Knowledge: Select three content-area (disciplinary) texts that you have used in your classroom. Go through them and underline words that you think provide clues to the structure of the text: *sequence, comparison, causation, description,* and *problem-solution.*

Apply Your Knowledge: Ideally, select two informational texts on a science or history topic that children will be learning about within the next several weeks. Score each text using a 1–5 scale on the four bulleted features you have just read. How do the texts compare? Is one consistently more demanding in terms of "academic language" or does it depend on the bullet you are looking at? What does this analysis tell you about where EBs need the most support in the texts? How could you provide that support? Use this analysis for every text you select for your class.

Engaging in Close Reading

The CCSS emphasize the importance of children being able to accomplish close readings of text. This concept is a new one to most educators and perhaps one of the most discussed aspects of the Common Core. The main goal of close reading is to foster habits of mind that lead to accurate understanding, analysis of, and reflection upon the deep meaning of a text or oral presentation. Ideally, these understandings should expand and enrich children's personal world views. There are no preschool learning foundations that identify close reading as a goal, although preschool precursors for the practice can be identified. The methods for successfully engaging EB children in close reading are dictated, to a significant degree, by having clarity on its main goal. At its best, close reading is not an academic exercise—it is a peak experience honed with text. It is like a long-distance endurance run for comprehending and thinking. And just as a long-distance run must be built up to, so is the case with close reading. Less demanding and shorter practices to master the foundational skills that support close reading are necessary. Motivation or desire to accomplish the goal, which is the deep knowing of a discourse, is essential for children if they are going to have the engagement and perseverance they need to accomplish close reading. And of course, the demands of close reading for EB children will almost certainly be greater than those for English-fluent children. Both groups of children require a developmental, gradual, and incremental sequence of instruction in order to accomplish the endurance race of comprehending and thinking that is at the heart of close reading.

Close reading begins with ensuring that children have an initial basic understanding of text. If first-grader William does not understand what happened when Little Red Riding Hood found grandma in the bed or if preschooler Martha does not understand the metamorphosis of a butterfly mentioned in narrative and informational read-alouds, respectively, there is little chance that either of these children can consider the author's purpose, perform a character analysis, or compare butterfly development to human development. The use of guiding questions, story sequencing cards, retelling with pictures or to a partner, and pictures to show who, what, where, when, and why are examples of practices to build a basic understanding of the discourse. The use of short texts or selections and repeated readings of the discourse are especially useful as EB children begin to develop their close reading fitness via experiencing initial success. Choosing passages that are easier to decode will again free resources for close reading.

Teaching Practice 16: Begin close reading by establishing children's basic understanding of the oral or written discourse.

Close reading is challenging and motivation is necessary for students to meet the challenge. One of the most important initial steps for close reading success is to choose text that will interest children. Helping children recognize their accomplishment with small pieces of success will support their motivation. When the teacher Ms. Hedrick asks guiding questions about the character of Little Red Riding Hood, directs children to the relevant text, and affirms the value of their responses, their motivation to persevere in close reading activities is supported. Many more practices that you can enact to support children's motivation during close reading can be found in Chapter 8. Preschool teachers understand the value of repeated reading, and most will attest to the enjoyment children have as their familiarity with a story or informational book grows. Many of you would probably attest to the increasing sophistication of vocabulary and thinking evident in discussion and follow-up activities that come with repeated reading. Repeated book reading is an excellent precursor for later close reading. The important point is that initial reading should be devoted to developing basic understanding, followed by more thinking and analysis with subsequent readings. This comprehending and thinking advancement, or close reading, can be supported by teacher questioning, small-group discussion, dramatic play, and pictures.

Teaching Practice 17: Develop preschool precursors to close reading by repeated book reading that progresses from a basic understanding to more sophisticated vocabulary and thinking.

Teaching Practice 18: Help children learn the process of close reading by initially performing close reading with simple stories and stories that are easy to decode, and by rereading.

Teaching Practice 19: Select texts that children are deeply interested in for close readings or build their interest before reading.

Reading of Self-Selected Books

Educational Principle 2: Advocate for and devote resources to develop school and classroom libraries and other means for providing EBs with a variety of interesting and readable books for school and home use.

From kindergarten through 2nd grade, it is critical to offer beginners plenty of practice reading texts that they can read and that reward them for expending the required effort. Study after study over many years has shown that the amount of actual reading occurring in classrooms during reading instruction or other times is very limited. So much time is spent learning how to read and performing related practice exercises that children have little time to do the very activity that is the goal of all of the literacy instruction: reading. Engaging with extended blocks of text or connected oral language is essential for using comprehension and thinking processes. Preschool-age children can look at picture books and familiar books and construct stories with props and other materials to activate the mental processes to support comprehending and thinking with language and text. Rich classroom, school, and community libraries as sources of readable and desirable texts are especially important for those EBs, whose families may have limited ability to access books.

Teaching Practice 20: Make it a priority to provide opportunities for children to read, pretend read, or look at self-selected texts for extended periods of time.

THE PREK–GRADE 2 CONTINUUM: COMPREHENDING AND THINKING WITH LANGUAGE AND TEXT

The Simple View of Reading model characterizes skilled reading as the simple combination of listening comprehension and word reading ability. Thinking of reading comprehension as essentially listening comprehension operating through written language establishes an important perspective and continuity for developing a PreK–2 continuum for comprehending and thinking. It begins in the oral mode at PreK and becomes increasingly text-based as children gain word reading efficiency from kindergarten through grade 2. When preschooler Gilbert draws a picture of the teacher's sentence "The dog frolicked in the mud" or retells a four-sentence story about what a friend with whom he has been partnered during a large-group lesson likes to do at home, they are working on reading comprehension. The extensive use of oral discourse through discussion, teacher oral reading, multimedia presentations, and other oral practices is valuable for developing EBs' listening comprehension PreK–2. You can feel confident that teacher read-alouds can support comprehension and are not handicapping children's comprehension because the children are not reading the texts themselves. The extensive use of oral discourse through discussion, teacher oral reading, and multimedia presentations and language-enriched play is valuable for EBs at all levels.

CONNECTIONS TO THE COMMON CORE STATE STANDARDS AND PRESCHOOL LEARNING STANDARDS

The research on reading comprehension of EBs and the strategies identified in the Common Core are important for promoting text comprehension. Emerging evidence shows that preschool-age and kindergarten children, including EBs, can be taught comprehension strategies with carefully designed instruction. Visualizing, retelling, summarizing, and self-monitoring are among these important strategies, as discussed earlier in this chapter. The CCSS for K–2 identify the thinking processes *compare, evidence, retell, describe, reasons, same, different* repeatedly. Table 7.3 presents the comprehension and thinking standards for K–2 presented in the CCSS. Preschool standards very often identify story retelling as a standard for language development. This emphasis reveals a beneficial alignment between PreK and K–2.

The comprehension processes and sophisticated thinking (argumentation, reasoning, questioning, and presentation related to grade-level topics and texts) identified in the CCSS also have oral language precursors that can be taught in preschool classrooms. For example, two possible preschool oral activities include the following:

- Have students draw a picture of a very important event from a story and then explain why it was chosen to a few other students who speak the same home language (reasoning).
- Hold a class discussion in which the teacher or a child holds a large image of the Big Bad Wolf. Children can ask the wolf questions that "he" answers while holding the large wolf image (questioning).

Very encouraging evidence from recent studies identifies the fact that children can be taught about the text structures present in subject-matter learning emphasized in the CCSS (Williams et al., 2016). There is growing recognition in preschool standards and guidelines consistent with the CCSS of the importance and benefit of informational text for language and literacy achievement. The Common Core has led to great attention to higher-order thinking, close reading, and demanding text. The foundations that support these three competencies are equally essential for EBs' literacy achievement. However, PreK frameworks or the CCSS do not sufficiently stipulate the essential integration of foundation skills (alphabet, phonemic awareness, word decoding), language structure, and vocabulary for strong comprehending and thinking with language and text.

The Common Core and many preschool standards are silent on the type of instruction that most effectively enhances comprehension and thinking competencies. We have seen again that research indicates the methods and what should be taught to increase children's comprehending and thinking. Explicit teacher instructional methods to teach strategies such as visualization, retelling, and summarizing; guidance and practice on managing informational and narrative text and the structures characterizing them; and frequent reading of texts that students can efficiently read are recommended.

Table 7.3. Common Core Standards on Comprehension

	Key Ideas and Details	Craft and Structure	Integration of Knowledge and Ideas	Range of Reading and Text Complexity
	Questions	**Words and phrases**	**Illustration experiences**	**Text experiences**
Kindergarten	With help, ask and answer questions about details.	Ask and answer questions about unknown words.	With help, link illustrations to story.	Engage in group reading activities.
Grade 1	Ask and answer questions about key details.	Identify feelings and senses in words and phrases.	Use illustrations and detail to describe characters, settings, and events.	Read grade 1 prose and poetry.
Grade 2	Answer who, what, where, when, why, and how questions.	Describe how words and phrases identify rhythm and meaning.	Use illustrations and digital sources to show understanding of story elements.	Read literature in the grade 2–3 complexity band.
	Retelling	**Text features**	**Compare and Contrast**	
Kindergarten	With help, retell familiar stories, including key details.	Recognize common types of text.	With help, compare and contrast characters' actions.	
Grade 1	Retell stories, including key details and the main message.	Know the difference between stories and informational text.	Compare and contrast experiences of characters.	
Grade 2	Recount stories, including diverse cultures and using the central message.	Describe overall story structure, beginning, and ending.	Compare and contrast two or more versions of the same story.	
	Characters	**Point of View**		
Kindergarten	With help, identify characters, settings, and main events.	Name author and illustrator and what they do.		
Grade 1	Describe characters, setting, and events using key details.	Identify who is telling a story at different points.		
Grade 2	Describe characters' responses to events and challenges.	Show character differences by speaking in a different voice.		

Educational Principles From Chapter 7

1. Inform others at grade-level meetings and your site administrators about the potential difficulties for EBs associated with text complexity at grades K–2.
2. Advocate for and devote resources to develop school and classroom libraries and other means for providing EBs with a variety of interesting and readable books for school and home use.

Teaching Practices From Chapter 7

1. Provide instruction in language structure, word reading efficiency, vocabulary, and language comprehension strategies to support comprehension and thinking lessons.
2. Increase children's word reading efficiency.
3. Provide many listening comprehension activities with narrative and informational discourse.
4. Provide a comprehensive curriculum that includes significant learning about science, the arts, social studies, and math.
5. Use practices that ensure relevant background knowledge is developed or activated.
6. Keep the relationship of background knowledge to the oral or written discourse in focus during lessons.
7. Teach EBs to visualize, retell, and summarize oral and written discourse and to utilize these strategies during reading.
8. Teach EBs to monitor comprehension with carefully designed instruction that makes the abstraction of the concept and language to teach it more concrete.
9. Build a basic understanding of the oral or written discourse (story or informational text) prior to strategy application.
10. Teach children the vocabulary for and processes of comparing, retelling, describing, giving reasons, summarizing, and finding evidence.
11. Activate children's L1 for initial high-level thinking and comprehending exercises.
12. Evaluate and select text for the level of complexity appropriate for the learning goal of every lesson.
13. Teach children the five most common informational text structures.
14. Provide children access (oral, written, or digital) to the concepts, ideas, knowledge, experiences, and people within both narrative and informational discourse.

(*Teaching Practices,* Continued)

15. Read or have children read a complex text or text selection more than once.
16 Begin close reading by establishing children's basic understanding of the oral or written discourse.
17. Develop preschool precursors to close reading by repeated book reading that progresses from a basic understanding to more sophisticated vocabulary and thinking.
18. Help children learn the process of close reading by initially performing close reading with simple stories and stories that are easy to decode, and by rereading.
19. Select texts that children are deeply interested in for close readings or build their interest before reading.
20. Make it a priority to provide opportunities for children to read, pretend read, or look at self-selected texts for extended periods of time.

CHAPTER 8

Enhancing Engagement, Perseverance, and Challenge Seeking

Important Research Findings About Engagement, Perseverance, and Challenge Seeking

- All emergent bilinguals have an intrinsic motivation to be competent.
- Classroom and teacher characteristics and practices can influence children's engagement, perseverance, and challenge seeking.
- Individual differences among children in motivation for language and literacy develop as early as preschool and predict later language and literacy achievement.
- Children's thoughts and feelings about their language and literacy competence influences their engagement, perseverance, and challenge seeking.
- Perceived failure at language and literacy tasks powerfully impedes children's perseverance.
- Classroom practices that support effort, autonomy, and relatedness increase engagement, perseverance, and challenge seeking.
- Educational practices that proactively support perseverance for EBs are particularly important because EBs' achievement in language and literacy tasks relies on their developing English language competence.
- The research on motivation (engagement and perseverance) among young EBs is very limited.

Children's motivation influences their academic-related behaviors and achievement. Motivation is defined as a mental process that activates, directs, and sustains goal-directed behavior. Children's internal motivation is seen in these behaviors:

- Their willingness to engage in language and literacy learning and their focus/intensity while doing so
- Their perseverance in language and literacy learning, particularly when tasks are difficult
- Their eagerness to participate in challenging language and literacy learning

When preschooler Lucas is the first to take his seat on the carpet as the storybook reading session begins and he eagerly asks, "What is the name of the story for today?" followed by a brushing off of the hand that is tickling him from behind, he is demonstrating a strong willingness to engage and focus on language and literacy.

The Latin root of the word *motivation* means "to move." Essentially, then, motivation activates and sustains children's engagement and perseverance. Differences in literacy motivation are already emerging in preschool children, and may be quite firmly developed by the end of 2nd grade (Chang & Burns, 2005). Early differences in motivation among preschool and kindergarten children are predictive of later literacy achievement (Chapman, Tunmer, & Prochnow, 2000; Lepola, Poskiparta, Laakkonen, & Niemi, 2005). However, I want to point out that most of the research on motivation has involved children who are monolingual. Therefore, some caution is needed in applying the results to EBs. Nonetheless, studies with older individuals support the general similarity of motivation across different cultural groups.

Motivation and achievement influence each other (Guthrie & Wigfield, 2000). Language and literacy achievement leads to motivation, and language and literacy motivation leads to achievement. If a student is highly motivated to learn to read and write, her achievement is likely to be boosted. If she has low motivation for language and literacy, her achievement is likely to be lowered. As is the case for many of the competencies related to literacy that are explored in other chapters in this book, preschool is an important window of opportunity for EBs to develop the thoughts and feelings that can sustain their effort in PreK–2 when the words used by teachers and encountered in text are difficult to understand, the ideas challenging and foreign, and the pages to be read and comprehended are many.

Uncovering the ways children think and feel about doing things, and documenting the behaviors that occur because of them, and the practices in schools and homes that shape these thoughts and feelings have all been the work of researchers who study motivation (Dweck, 1975; Guthrie & Wigfield, 2000; Harter, 1974, 1978). Figure 8.1 summarizes what has been learned through this research. The goal of this chapter is to share what has been learned and to help you develop practices that will increase EBs' engagement, perseverance, and challenge seeking during language and literacy learning.

Children's thoughts and feelings about literacy powerfully shape their engagement, perseverance, and challenge-seeking—their motivation. Thoughts related to the question "Will I be successful?" are particularly influential when it comes to motivation. In classrooms, children are receiving information related to this question every single day, if not during every single activity. Feelings related to the questions "Does this matter to me?" and "Do I like it?" are also particularly influential on children's motivation (Harter, 1974; Schiefele, 2001). In this chapter, you will learn how children's answers to these questions affect how they think and feel about themselves and about language and literacy. You will also learn about the characteristics of schools and classrooms that have their own independent and unique relationship to engagement and perseverance. There may be some surprises in store.

Figure 8.1. What Classroom Practices Influence Children's Motivation?

- Teacher praise and evaluation
- Extent of comparisons among children
- What children learn about ability and effort
- Opportunity for collaboration
- Interesting oral and written text
- Children's evidence of their competence
- Children experiencing both autonomy and relatedness

But first, think about an EB child in your classroom whom you consider motivated for language and literacy. Think of another child you would consider much less motivated. What did you base your selections on? I would guess that you might have chosen "stick-with-it-ness" and "active participation" as two key characteristics that differentiate the two children you selected. Indeed, these two characteristics that are often identified by teachers are found in the list taken from research (e.g. Dweck, 1986; Eccles & Wigfield, 2002) and shown in Figure 8.2.

There are many different theories of motivation. Those selected for inclusion in this chapter are Competence Motivation, Mastery and Performance Motivation, and Self-Determination Theory. These three theories of motivation can guide understanding of how differences among children in motivation have been and are shaped by school experiences.

COMPETENCE MOTIVATION THEORY

Every Child's Need for Competence and Mastery

Educational Principle 1: Believe that all children have an inborn need to learn and be competent.

In 1959, Robert White wrote a paper titled "Motivation Reconsidered: The Concept of Competence" that revolutionized the study of motivation. Previously, differences in motivation had been explained on the basis of the rewards or punishments that were received for engaging in a particular activity. It was believed that children would read because they were given stickers or A grades, had their name posted on a board, received teacher praise, or were recognized at an assembly. In other words, motivation was shaped and learned according to whether rewards or punishing consequences followed children's actions.

White turned this thinking on its head. He argued that humans, including children, have an inborn need to be competent in their environment. They have an inherent need to explore and experiment with their environment, to achieve an understanding of it, and to acquire the competencies that support adaptation to it. All

Figure 8.2. Characteristics of Children Highly Motivated and Less Motivated for Language and Literacy Learning

Highly Motivated	Less Motivated
Choose language arts activities	Avoid language arts activities
Stick with language arts activities	Give up quickly or hurry to finish
Focus attention and work with diligence	Are distractible and off task
Seek help when they have difficulty	Give up or attempt to cover up when they have difficulty
Tell themselves to try harder or try differently when they are unsuccessful	Tell themselves that they are incapable or not smart when they are unsuccessful
Prefer tasks that are a little challenging	Prefer tasks that are easy
Have positive emotions about language and literacy activities	Have negative emotions and anxiety about language and literacy activities

children are born with the tools of curiosity and inclination for exploration in their quest to become competent, or effective, in their environment.

CLASSROOM PRACTICES TO SPARK CHILDREN'S NEED FOR COMPETENCE

Educational Principle 2: Provide professional development that explains the competence assessment biases that teachers may have.

When implemented in your classroom, the following learning conditions will spark curiosity:

- Moderate challenge
- Causality (a child makes something happen rather than watching someone else make it happen)
- Novelty
- Mystery, anomaly
- Strong personal interest/relevance

When children are presented activities that may be difficult for them initially but that they can achieve with practice and several tries, moderate challenge is introduced. When children do an experiment with mixing colors rather than watching the teacher do it, they experience causality. When new materials are introduced to the dramatic play center, novelty is created. Mystery and anomaly, and strong personal interest/relevance, are illustrated in the following anecdote:

> At a family picnic, preschool teachers observed that EB children played games with a pair of sticks and a variety of ball-like items (cloth rags, orange, small

> ball, pods from trees). The items could be tossed, flipped up off the ground, or rolled along with the sticks with amazing skill. The teachers then brought the ball and stick games into the classroom and used them to study weight and gravity.

This practice was a lovely demonstration of creating conditions of strong personal interest and relevance, as well as the type of integration of cultural funds of knowledge discussed in Chapter 1. The teachers not only enhanced children's motivation but also demonstrated that they valued family and community funds of knowledge.

Teaching Practice 1: Plan language and literacy activities that release and engage children's curiosity through moderate challenge, causality, novelty, mystery/anomaly, and strong personal interest/relevance.

> *Apply Your Knowledge:* Take a science or social studies lesson that you have taught recently. Go through it and verify any parts of it that show the conditions for sparking curiosity listed above. Add brief modifications showing how you could add *moderate challenge, causality, novelty, mystery/anomaly,* and *strong personal interest/relevance.*

It may have occurred to you that many of the external rewarding practices that White's theory took aim at continue to be used in PreK–2 programs—more so in K–2. Recognition assemblies for meeting grade-level CCSS benchmarks, certificates for being a good classroom helper, and treasure boxes where children can redeem points earned for good behaviors and grades are all examples of these practices, which are very likely to distract children from their competence motivation. There are better practices that teachers can use to implement their genuine interest in supporting children's self-sustaining motivation for language and literacy. The research described in Figure 8.3 summarizes an experiment showing that success-only learning was less effective for helping children who had come to believe that they were unable to do math than was helping them change their thinking about the value of effort.

Another idea of the Competence Theory of Motivation mentioned in the previous section is that tasks that are moderately challenging will most strongly activate competence motivation. The term *moderately challenging* means there is a possibility of task success but there is also some risk of being unsuccessful or perhaps even of failing. Easy tasks or tasks that are too hard do not have the potential to advance competence because guaranteed success (too easy) or failure (too difficult) don't change competence. Additional practice with naming alphabet letters for a child who already knows them, or trying to do a close reading of a text that has vocabulary so difficult it is incomprehensible, will not activate competence motivation. A

Figure 8.3. Learned Helplessness Experiment

> Children with learned helplessness—who had extreme reactions to any kind of math failure, giving up almost completely—participated in one of two math interventions. One group of children worked on math problems that were very carefully selected to ensure that the children would be able to work them successfully. The other group of children was given carefully selected problems that they could not work and finish, and these children were taught to tell themselves that trying harder would help. After training, children in the success-only treatment group continued to experience severe performance deterioration after failure. Children in the treatment where they had some failure and were then taught to think about the value of effort rather than their low ability, either maintained or improved their performance—and the change occurred with only 25 short lessons (Dweck, 1975).

recent review of kindergarten learning concluded that more challenging reading content led to higher academic achievement than did easier material (Claessens, Engel, & Curran, 2014). Educators who work with young children sometimes emphasize success-only learning, or worry that challenges and initial setbacks will frustrate young children too much. Kids are up to the challenge, and moderate challenge will actually benefit their motivation. Challenge for EBs may be especially important because of evidence that teachers underestimate by about 17% kindergarten children's actual levels or reading ability when they come from families with low socioeconomic status in low-income and low-achieving schools (Ready & Wright, 2011).

Teaching Practice 2: Provide children with language and literacy learning opportunities that are moderately challenging.

A third major idea of the Competence or Effectance Theory of Motivation is that when humans, including PreK–2 children, perceive that they have increased their competence, they experience pleasure (Harter, 1974). Think of the child who has just taken his or her first proud steps. The child is likely to smile or laugh to express delight. The child needs no reward or pat on the back to walk more or feel good about his or her competence to do so. Accomplishment—perceived by the child as increasing his or her competence, not as perceived by parents, teachers, or others—leads to the kind of pleasure associated with competence motivation. Thus, when competence motivation is turned on and children perceive that they have increased their competence, the accomplishment itself is rewarding.

The idea of competence motivation is a powerful way of thinking about what gets children to act with positive engagement, perseverance, and challenge seeking. First, it calls attention to the underlying engine for competence that is present in all children in the classroom. This engine is humming along, looking for experiences where a child will think, "This will help me adapt to my environment" and move it into gear. Further, when teachers possess an understanding of competence motivation and observe non-engagement or other behaviors that are not an expression of competence motivation, they will be encouraged to wonder, "How can this activity turn on this need for competence?" rather than perhaps attributing children's behaviors to practices in the home or the personal shortcomings of the child. The idea of competence motivation has a very special relevance to EBs because it shifts attention to adapting to children and the unique and special circumstances that signal competence to them. Thus, motivation research establishes yet again the benefits of school language and literacy activity that has personal relevance and interest, and ties into valued prior experiences.

Teaching Practice 3: Let learning be its own reward, particularly when children value the activity and have the expectation that they can succeed at it.

MASTERY AND PERFORMANCE MOTIVATION THEORY

> ***Apply Your Knowledge:*** Select an EB in your classroom you consider less motivated for language and literacy learning. List the evidence for your assessment. Go back to Figure 8.2 that shows the characteristics of less motivated children. Which of these characteristics does the child have? Now, imagine that you are a competence motivation expert. How would you explain the characteristics showing lack of motivation in the child you selected? List two things you could try to turn on the competence motivation engine for language and literacy learning. Try them out.

Patterns of Motivation

The concept of competence motivation triggered interest in children's mental workings that could suppress or activate the need to be competent in particular areas. Motivation researchers became curious about how children's thoughts and feelings about activities such as reading would influence their engagement, perseverance, and challenge-seeking behaviors (Harter, 1978). Researchers found that children had two types of mental processes that were very influential on motivation behaviors (Atkinson, 1964; Guthrie & Wigfield, 2000:

- Thoughts that children had about their ability and the likelihood that they would be successful at some task
- Feelings and emotions related to how much the task was valued, liked, and associated with positive emotions such as pride and pleasure

Two patterns of motivation with enormous consequences for children's classroom motivation were identified (Dweck, 1986). One of these patterns was a *maladaptive* one that was associated with disengaging, giving up, and experiencing negative emotions such as fear, anxiety, and shame when presented with a task where the maladaptive pattern was present. This pattern is called a *performance orientation.* The other pattern was an *adaptive* one that was associated with fortified effort and perseverance, and experiencing positive emotions like hopefulness for success and pleasure in doing the task. This pattern is called a *mastery orientation.* Refer to Figure 8.2 for examples of several of the thinking and learning behaviors associated with the two patterns.

I hope that you are exercising curiosity as part of your competence motivation toward developing your expertise as a teacher of EBs and are wondering how these two different patterns develop. Children do not exhibit these different patterns as a simple manifestation of their nature, character, or grit. Characteristics of schools and classrooms, and the practices within them, play a powerful role in the development of these two orientations.

How Children's Thinking and Feeling Lead to Mastery and Performance Orientations to Language and Literacy

Educational Principle 3: Help children have hope for success and perceive that language and literacy learning has adaptive value.

Classroom practices shape children's mastery and performance patterns of motivation for language and literacy primarily through their influence on two aspects of

Apply Your Knowledge: You are probably starting to get the idea of how the two patterns of motivation are different. Try this exercise to clarify the distinctions. Write the headings Performance Orientation and Mastery Orientation on a sheet of paper. Place the words from the following jumble in the correct column. Try to pair each phrase with its appropriate opposite in the other column.

Prefers challenge

Avoids challenge

Believe ability cannot change

Wants to look smart

Pessimistic and thinks about avoiding failure

Believe their ability can change

Optimistic and thinks about achieving success

Focuses on improvement

children's mental processes. The first aspect is children's thoughts and assessments about their language and literacy ability and the likelihood that they can and will be successful at these tasks. The second aspect is affective—that is, having to do with emotions and feelings. It relies on the extent to which children value language and literacy learning and find it emotionally rewarding and even pleasurable.

In Figure 8.4, meet Raul, Yang, Katy, and Ixyanna, whose interpretations of a difficult literacy task illustrate the thinking and feeling aspects of mastery and performance orientations. All four students are novice learners of English. They are in 2nd grade and have read the story of Little Red Riding Hood. They are all having difficulty with the assignment to find text evidence showing that the Big Bad Wolf is, indeed, bad. Compare how Raul and Yang think about ability and the likelihood of their success. Katy and Ixyanna illustrate the affective component of mastery (adaptive) and performance (maladaptive) orientations. Compare how Katy and Ixyanna feel about reading and the story and the how much they value the "finding evidence" activity.

One of the challenges for motivation researchers (and teachers) is to figure out a way to "see" these thoughts, values, and feelings that children experience. Two methods used by researchers are as follows:

1. Preschool-age children are taught to use a line of grouped stars to indicate how much they like to eat ice cream and how fast a runner they are. Then they are told to select the group of stars that shows how good they are at reading (ability perception). Next, they are asked to pick the group of stars that shows how much they like to read (valuing of reading).
2. Second-graders are given a list of statements. Underneath each is a large number 1, 2, and 3. Each child is asked to read each statement and choose the number that best describes him or her. Examples: "I am good at reading;" "When reading is hard, I work harder;" "When reading is hard, I want to do something else;" "Reading makes me feel good;" "Reading makes me feel unhappy."

After reading about these methods, challenge yourself to come up with ways to figure out the competence/ability and valuing/affective thoughts and feelings of the EB children in your classroom.

Teaching Practice 4: Find out what children think about their language and literacy ability and how much they value language and literacy learning.

Classroom Practices to Foster Mastery Motivation

Educational Principle 4: Limit the use of schoolwide programs that promote comparisons among children.

Children may enter your classroom with adaptive mastery motivation or maladaptive performance motivation patterns forming and sometimes already formed to a

Figure 8.4. Mental Processes of Mastery and Performance Patterns

Thoughts About Ability and Expectations for Success	Feelings and Valuing
Raul Raul's thinking about ability and his chances for success goes like this: "I am a pretty good reader." When he has difficulty finding text evidence, he tells himself, "I can get better at finding evidence" and "I will keep looking at the pages until I find some evidence." Raul believes he can increase his ability at finding evidence through effort and mindful activity. He has a reservoir of positive expectation from which he can draw to help him try again and work longer and harder when the going gets tough. Raul's thoughts about ability and expectations for success suggest a mastery-oriented motivation pattern.	**Katy** Katy's feeling toward and valuing of the difficult task goes like this: "Oh boy, I really like this story. It is a little scary and that makes it exciting. When we got to tell about a time we were afraid of something, it helped me like the story more. I want to get that Big Bad Wolf with evidence. Evidence can really show your idea. I feel good and proud when I find evidence." These lifted positive feelings about reading, her excitement and enjoyment of the story, and her positive valuing of finding evidence help her engage, persevere, and seek challenge on a difficult task. Katy's feelings and valuing suggest a mastery-oriented motivation pattern.
Yang Yang thinks differently from Raul about the difficult task. Yang's thinking goes like this: "I am not a good reader" and "Other kids are much better readers than I am." He also thinks, "No matter what I do, I won't ever be a good reader. You have to be a good reader to show the teacher you can find evidence." Yang is thinking that his reading ability is stable; it will not change. He believes it matters little how hard he tries; he just doesn't have the right stuff. He has low expectations for success because he believes that his low ability is something that he can't change. He focuses on showing the teacher that he is a good reader rather than on actually finding evidence. He looks at just a few lines on the first page and then begins to aggravate his neighbor. He never finds the evidence. The way he thinks about ability is strengthened and will undermine his effort when he encounters the next difficulty. Yang's thoughts about ability and expectations for success suggest a performance-oriented motivation toward literacy.	**Ixyanna** Ixyanna's feelings toward and valuing of the difficult task is very different from Katy's. Ixyanna's feelings and emotions go like this: "This is a story for babies and I don't like reading baby stories. Everybody knows the Big Bad Wolf is bad because everybody already knows this dumb story. Why is the teacher making us look for evidence, then? And it is so hard, so hard. Ugh! This is so boring, just like the other stories we read." She has a negative emotional response to the task and does not value reading stories much. She is unlikely to engage, persevere, and seek challenge in literacy learning. Ixyanna's feelings and valuing suggest a performance-oriented motivation pattern.

> *Apply Your Knowledge:* Write two questions you could ask children to get an inside look at how they think about their ability for a language or literacy goal you are currently working on in your class. Next, write two questions you could ask children to get an inside look at how they value the same instructional goal.

significant degree by previous home, community, and schooling experiences. When the emerging pattern is the adaptive, mastery orientation, you have much to capitalize upon. But in cases where children enter with a maladaptive or performance orientation, you can begin to reshape that pattern.

There are three main categories of classroom practices, almost completely under teachers' control, that can powerfully shape children's thoughts about their ability and their feelings about the value and desirability of language and literacy tasks:

1. The messages that children receive about their language and literacy ability through teacher praise and feedback
2. Student evaluation practices
3. The extent and nature of social comparison among children

You have a powerful motivation-determining tool in the nature of the praise and feedback comments used in your classroom. Certain kinds of praise and feedback will support engagement, perseverance, and challenge seeking. You won't be surprised to read that the effects of praise and feedback depend on how they shape children's thinking about and valuing of language and literacy achievement (see Figure 8.5). You may initially find that it takes effort to monitor and change the verbal comments you make to children. As the balance of comments increases in the motivation-enhancing direction, using comments to increase motivation will just happen as easily as saying "good job."

Evaluation practices also influence the development of students' mastery or performance orientations. When second-grader Meeta has the opportunity to correct

> *Apply Your Knowledge:* Take a moment to gather some information on how you use verbal praise and feedback in your classroom.
>
> » When and why do you praise children or give them feedback on their work?
>
> » Make a short list of the verbal praise and feedback statements you use frequently.
>
> » Keep your answers in mind as you read the next section.

Figure 8.5. Effects on Motivation of Teacher Praise and Feedback Comments

PROMOTES MASTERY ORIENTATION		PROMOTES PERFORMANCE ORIENTATION	
Category	**Example**	**Category**	**Example**
Recognizes effort	You are learning because you are practicing.	Recognizes ability	Smart girls learn the letters like you have.
Attributes success to effort	You named all of the letters. You tried hard.	Attributes success to ability	You named all of the letters. You are so smart.
Focuses attention on task-oriented behavior	You are listening and looking at the pictures. You should be proud of yourself.	Focuses attention on teacher approval	I like how you are listening to the story and looking at the pictures.
Recognizes meaningful growth and improvement	Last time you had 40 words per minute. This time you read 45 words per minute.	Recognizes absolute achievement	You met the fluency benchmark. You are a good reader.
Is individual and specific	Wow. I really enjoyed reading your story because it had so many describing words.	Is uniform and global	Good job (after reading story). Nice job writing.
Fosters the idea that children put out effort for their own reasons	This story shows you really want to express yourself when you write.	Fosters the idea that children put out effort to please others	Your parents will be so proud of this story.
Given for significant achievement	I heard you decode two-syllable words.	Given for minimal or easy achievement	Nice—you have your book out.

the spelling errors the teacher has marked on her story or to lengthen it by having more time to work on it, she is learning the value of effort. Revision and more work is unlikely to lead to more motivation if the child perceives these efforts to be a punishment. There is an important distinction between the teacher saying, "I have shown you where the spelling errors are on your story; go correct them and your story will have interesting ideas and correct writing" and saying, "You weren't careful when you wrote the story; now you have to go back and do it over." When children can set goals for improvement (with some true sense that they have been involved in a negotiation) and then track progress toward it, they are having a personal and powerful demonstration of improvement and mastery. Children who understand that a Common Core standard for their grade is to learn common pronouns and they have learned two out of five are more likely to develop a mastery orientation compared to a punitive orientation regarding not meeting standards where they are told, "You will have to go to reading intervention over winter break because you didn't meet the standards."

Teaching Practice 5: Consistently use praise and evaluation practices that orient children to effort, improvement, specific accomplishment, positive feelings, and personal agency.

The final category of teacher practices that influence motivation includes those practices related to social comparison. It is an undeniable and arguably unfortunate fact that placing children of similar ages in classrooms creates inevitable social comparison. First-grader Orion hears Edward reading much more quickly than he does and concludes that Edward is the better reader. When those inevitabilities are downplayed, children's optimism for their own competence can be sustained more easily. Conversely, when teacher practice shines a bright light on these comparisons by promoting them, students' sense of competence may be damaged. The guiding principle for classroom practice is a simple one: Create learning conditions and classroom practices that do not easily allow for social comparison. Guided reading, round-robin reading, performances in front of other children, allowing children to choose groups or the next child to get a turn, stamping different colors on papers based on quality, posting the best student work, or public progress charts for individual achievement of CCSS are all circumstances where young children's academic and social competence may be compared to others. This shared knowledge leads students to compare themselves with others rather than focusing on their own growth and effort. When public knowledge is further bolstered by teacher comments that signal some children are better than others, there is potential for a combined assault. Social comparisons are triggered when the teacher rings a bell and announces, "Galilea just hit the fluency benchmark" or "I really like how Michael is listening." Young EBs are particularly vulnerable to negative academic comparison because they very often will be behind English fluent children on tasks that require substantial levels of English proficiency.

Teaching Practice 6: Create environments that do not easily allow for social comparison.

SELF-DETERMINATION THEORY

Children's Need for Competence, Relatedness, and Autonomy

The third and final theory of motivation that I have selected because of its relevance to EBs and classroom practice is Self-Determination Theory (Reeve, Deci, & Ryan, 2004). Within this theory, children are believed to have three needs that, when satisfied, contribute to motivation: *competence, relatedness,* and *autonomy* (see Figure 8.6). Let's return now to the assignment related to *Little Red Riding Hood*, in which children successfully find their choice of any piece of evidence that shows the Big Bad Wolf is a nasty fellow and then work with two buddies to make a chart combining their evidence. In this assignment, children's needs for competence, autonomy, and relatedness are all met to some degree.

Figure 8.6. The Three Needs of Self-Determination

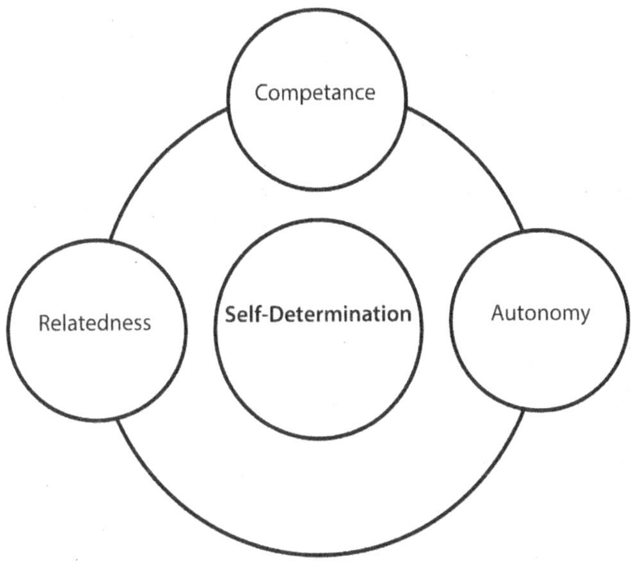

The relationship of competence to motivation has already been discussed in the previous sections. Its appearance yet again in Self-Determination Theory highlights its central role in motivation. The discussion of Self-Determination Theory in this section is limited to the needs of autonomy and relatedness.

What does it mean to have autonomy within a classroom setting? There are surely limits on autonomy because there is a specific course of study and coexistence with a large group of other people is necessary. Webster's dictionary defines *autonomy* as "the quality or state of being self-governing." The core feature of autonomy is the perception that there is some measure of the right to self-determine a course of action.

Relatedness refers to connections with others that are emotionally rewarding. A synonym is *belongingness*. The need for relatedness is fulfilled by direct interactions with others where there is a shared, positive sense of togetherness. This need for relatedness can be met by teachers, other adults, and peers. Satisfying the need for relatedness is not dependent upon liking or friendship, although these conditions may enhance it. Children may even experience relatedness when they are doing independent work, with the understanding that the teacher and peers are available for sharing and assistance.

Classroom Practices to Foster Self-Determination

Educational Principle 5: Enroll EBs in clusters within classrooms, taking into account shared language and culture.

Autonomy can be supported by providing children some choice in topics, procedures, and how projects are to be demonstrated. Preschool programs have long appreciated the importance of choice; Head Start guidelines even specify that children must have daily free choice. For kindergarten through grade 2 EBs, an important way to support autonomy is through the practice of a regular independent reading program where children always choose what they read. Praise and verbal comments focusing children's attention on the personal reasons for acting and doing may also increase their sense of autonomy (for example, "You like to write new words in your personal dictionary. You are doing things that matter to you"). Autonomy and, hence, motivation can also be promoted by attributing students' learning to their own efforts ("Wow, you worked really hard on drawing a picture of the story") and their engagement to their own motivation ("Today when you were listening so hard to the story, I could see you want to learn English"). A learner-focused classroom that encourages and allows independence in solving learning and social problems can also help children feel autonomous or self-determining. Actively drawing upon children's interests and experiences is an important practice that can contribute to children's sense of self-direction and autonomy. When Eriberto believes "In my class we learn about things I am interested in and my teachers and classmates care about what I think," his personal power to influence his learning—his autonomy—is bolstered.

Teaching Practice 7: Allow children extensive independent reading and choice of the texts to be read.

Teaching Practice 8: Provide choice in language and literacy learning topics, activities, procedures, and products.

Relatedness can be fostered in collaborative groups. However, simply being in a cooperative or collaborative group does not ensure it. When children are in groups with high levels of disagreement or when there are dynamics establishing status hierarchies among children, relatedness may even be damaged. These status hierarchies can occur when EBs are grouped with English-proficient children in classrooms where the superiority and desirability of English is ever present and is associated with children's perceptions of what and who is valued. An emotionally warm classroom climate; an accessible, understanding, and helpful teacher; and a spirit of helping and comradeship among children is the essence of relatedness. A shared classroom identity that celebrates similarities while recognizing differences contributes to relatedness. The presence of other children who speak the same language and are encouraged to use that language together may also increase relatedness.

Teaching Practice 9: Use collaborative learning groups where positive relationships among children are planned and monitored.

> *Apply Your Knowledge*: Make and implement a plan to increase in your class children's sense of shared identity, positive relationships, and opportunities to connect with others during language and literacy learning.

FURTHER THOUGHTS ABOUT MOTIVATION

Child Perceptions of Low Academic Ability and Failure: A Very Special Worry

Children's perception that they have low ability in language and literacy learning is the most motivation-damaging thought they can have. It can be damaging even if objective criteria reveal competence. If Ramon thinks he is not good at reading because he is not smart enough or is incapable of learning, it will be very hard for him to engage, persevere, or seek challenge—he'll believe there is no point to it because nothing can change. When children with a tendency toward this type of thought process encounter perceived or actual academic failure, such as not achieving standards or not being able to answer when asked a question during book reading, their motivation will be seriously suppressed. Over time, a pattern develops where children no longer engage or try.

It is undoubtedly the case that all children will encounter tasks and activities that are difficult for them. In fact, you learned how moderate challenges activate competence motivation, how challenge helps children learn the value of effort, and how challenging content gives young children the opportunity to learn more (Claessens, Engel, & Curran, 2014). The very definition of a moderate challenge recognizes that failure is a possibility. Mastery motivation theory recognizes the value of nonsuccess indirectly because nonsuccess or difficulty invokes thoughts about the value of effort and renewed vigor—a stalwart part of adaptive motivation.

Teaching Practice 10: Monitor and control the amount of perceived failure children experience.

Teaching Practice 11: Break tasks into parts according to difficulty, where success on easier portions can balance failures on more difficult portions.

Teaching Practice 12: Allow children to correct and improve work, turning possible failures into successes thorough effort.

I do not know of any research on the effect of failure on PreK–2 EBs. But when children have repeated failures with limited or no opportunity to turn failure into success and/or attribute those failures to low ability and perceive that there are consequences for failure (such as not meeting standards or receiving low grades), they are in serious motivational difficulty. There is a strong possibility that EBs will be

Figure 8.7. How to Collaborate with Families in Helping Their Emergent Bilingual Children Engage, Persevere, and Seek Challenge

- Help families understand that how they praise and provide correction to their children can influence how much children engage and how hard they try in language and literacy learning.
- Provide families with specific suggestions on how they can praise children for success, including the following:
  - ✓ Praise for effort
  - ✓ Praise for solving challenging tasks
  - ✓ Tell children they should be proud of themselves.
- Encourage families to have children work regularly together with them, siblings, family members, or others within the community on everyday projects (such as cooking a meal, washing a car, and so forth).
- Help families provide choices for children.
- Encourage families to allow their children to do some things that are difficult for them and then help them to overcome difficulties.
- Discourage families from using extrinsic rewards for activities that children should enjoy and value on their own (such as team sports, completing homework, and so on).

at risk for these motivational consequences because of the likelihood that they will experience repeated academic challenges. Educators are urged to control the amount of failure that EBs experience and help them see difficulty as a call to effort rather than a crushing perception of low ability. Teachers can also reach out to the families of EBs to help them develop positive motivation (see Figure 8.7).

Teaching Practice 13: Help children learn to invoke more effort and practice when they perceive that they have failed.

A Key to the Castle: Learning Language of Motivation

There is specific language that will help EBs think about motivation and respond positively to the motivation-enhancing practices of their teachers. They will need language related to the thinking processes and the emotional, valuing aspects of language and literacy achievement. Figure 8.8 contains many of these words. There are probably more that you can add to these two categories. The next **Apply Your Knowledge** exercise asks you to think further about the language of motivation.

Teaching Practice 14: Teach children the thinking-related and emotional/valuing vocabulary related to motivation.

Figure 8.8. The Language of Motivation

Thinking Processes Language		Emotional and Valuing Language
Ability	Overcome	Important
Effort	Persevere	Interest
Success	Help	Independent
Challenge		Happy
Goal		Exciting
Improvement		Belonging
Criteria		Proud
Reason		Like
Failure		Unhappy

Characteristics of Cultural Groups, Communities, Schools, and Classrooms Relating to Motivation

Educational Principle 6: View the diversity within schools as an asset and capitalize on the benefits of connecting children with others of the same group(s).

> *Apply Your Knowledge:* Which of the Language of Motivation words do you think would be best to start with for PreK? Which might be better for kindergarten? For grade 1? For grade 2? How can you teach these somewhat abstract and complex concepts? How could you use children's first language to help?

The characteristics of the social groups that children are embedded within are associated with children's motivation for literacy and for engagement, perseverance, and challenge-seeking behaviors. Cross-cultural studies show that the thoughts children use to answer the questions "How good am I at____?" and the feelings that answer the question "How much do I value or like _____?" matter for motivation. However, in most studies, children are older than PreK–2.

In general, relatedness is important for motivation and academic achievement across many cultural groups and communities. Cultural groups vary in the extent to which they value autonomy and relatedness. Here is a focal point, though—the valuing of each is important (Markus & Kitayama, 1991). The stereotype that mainstream EF children are individualistic while other groups are collectivist is too simple. Because learning occurs within each child, knowing the differences between children in your classroom rather than between groups is essential. Be careful not to make it too simple!

School and classroom characteristics related to motivation include the percentage of EBs in the school and classroom, and being in a group with ethnically and linguistically similar others. It may be surprising to hear that schools with more diversity and the presence of peers of the same race/ethnicity are associated with positive socioemotional and academic development (Benner & Crosnoe, 2011). Other researchers have reported the motivational benefits of being in classrooms with higher numbers of EBs for 9th-grade language-minority students (Rjosk, Richter, Hochweber, Lüdtke, & Stanat, 2015). The study suggested that emotional connections to peers may be especially important to EBs.

Here is an example of class assignment practices in which these important grouping factors were not considered. In one school, the perceived level of English proficiency and work habits of EBs were identified by kindergarten teachers on colored cards. Class lists for the following year were made by distributing the cards in such a way that each teacher "got his or her fair share" of children at each level. Each of the five 1st-grade teachers was assigned about five EBs. There was no consideration of home languages, friendships, or family circumstances in forming those clusters.

Yet another factor leading to increased persistence and learning—the labeling of task groups—was studied by Master and Walton (2013). They found that when 4-year-old children belonged to groups where the group had a name related to accomplishing the assigned task, they were highly motivated. For example, the *evidence detectives group* looked for evidence in the text, the *retell wizards group* summarized text for the class, or the *vocabulary masters group* found and explained challenging vocabulary within a text. In contrast, the children in groups simply labeled 1, 2, or 3 were less engaged. What a small but significant change!

Teaching Practice 15: Group together children of similar languages and similar ethnic groups for some activities.

THE PREK–GRADE 2 CONTINUUM: ENHANCING MOTIVATION

Children's motivation for literacy and other academic subjects changes with age (Chapman & Tunmer, 1997; Dweck, 2002; Eccles, Wigfield, Harold, & Blumenfeld, 1993). Unfortunately, the typical pattern is one of motivational decline. Young children tend to overestimate their competence, to be quite optimistic about their future performance, and to express positive valuing of school-like tasks (Stipek, Roberts, & Sanborn, 1984). Toddlers and preschool children begin to develop self-evaluations of their abilities based on their performance and feedback from others. The relatively high level of preschool motivation declines between early and middle elementary school, and declines further into the middle school period (Eccles et al., 1993; Wigfield, Eccles, Roesser, & Schiefele, 2008). This change with age has been explained by the following:

- Classroom practices related to teacher feedback, evaluation, and autonomy support
- Level of interestingness, meaningfulness, and personalization of curriculum and learning tasks
- Children's experience with peers and schooling
- Children's growing cognitive capacities, leading to more accurate self-perceptions of competence

You have learned how this pattern of decline may be halted by best practices related to praise, evaluation, social comparison, and the use of motivation-supporting grouping.

PreK programs have a long history of valuing and emphasizing the importance of self-determination through the autonomy afforded by choice activities and support for relatedness through practices to promote social–emotional well-being. However, the importance of competence, particularly in the context of academic achievement, has been undervalued in many preschool programs.

CONNECTIONS TO THE COMMON CORE STATE STANDARDS AND PRESCHOOL LEARNING STANDARDS

A number of standards within the Common Core may be especially consequential for EBs' motivation because they may be very difficult for EBs to achieve. If this is the case, there is the worrisome possibility that EB children will experience all of the negative motivational effects of real or perceived failure. Reading of grade-level and complex text, learning subject-matter vocabulary and concepts in English, and using English to express argumentation and other types of abstract and complex thinking are some of the standards that are likely to carry increased risk of failure for EBs. You have learned about the special and deep motivational consequences of children's perceived failure because it so strongly threatens their sense of competence.

The manner in which progress monitoring and its consequences occur and the determination and consequences of making adequate yearly progress are also pressure points for EBs' motivational outcomes. These practices can:

- threaten children's sense of competence,
- contribute to children thinking that how smart they are delimits their academic success,
- create feelings of anxiety and dislike,
- detract from the capacity of schools to satisfy children's need for relatedness and autonomy, and
- be held over children's heads to satisfy the expectations of parents, teachers, or administrators.

If these things happen, children will be distanced from developing or drawing upon their potential inner motivational resources. On the other hand, the emphasis on collaboration in presentations, forming arguments, and so on may support motivation by enhancing EBs' sense of relatedness. Collaborative groups that include others of similar ethnic or language background may also enhance motivation.

The activation of students' inner resources is at the core of adaptive motivation that is self-sustaining and emotionally positive. I am certain that this is the kind of motivation that powers engagement, perseverance, and challenge-seeking in language and literacy learning that teachers desire for their students. There is adequate research on motivation to guide teachers in implementing classroom practices that will help PreK–2 EB children engage, persevere, and seek challenges in language and literacy learning. The classroom practices discussed in this chapter are almost entirely under your control to implement. There are no special materials required. Lengthy professional development is not needed to increase and hone the use of these practices. It doesn't cost a penny. You can start tomorrow. Your emergent bilinguals will be glad that you did.

Educational Principles From Chapter 7

1. Believe that all children have an inborn need to learn and be competent.
2. Provide professional development that explains the competence assessment biases that teachers may have.
3. Help children have hope for success and perceive that language and literacy learning has adaptive value.
4. Limit the use of schoolwide programs that promote comparisons among children.
5. Enroll EBs in clusters within classrooms, taking into account shared language and culture.
6. View the diversity within schools as an asset and capitalize on the benefits of connecting children with others of the same group(s).

Teaching Practices From Chapter 7

1. Plan language and literacy activities that release and engage children's curiosity through moderate challenge, causality, novelty, mystery/anomaly, and strong personal interest/relevance.
2. Provide children with language and literacy learning opportunities that are moderately challenging.
3. Let learning be its own reward, particularly when children value the activity and have the expectation that they can succeed at it.
4. Find out what children think about their language and literacy ability and how much they value language and literacy learning.
5. Consistently use praise and evaluation practices that orient children to effort, improvement, specific accomplishment, positive feelings, and personal agency.
6. Create environments that do not easily allow for social comparison.
7. Allow children extensive independent reading and choice of the texts to be read.
8. Provide choice in language and literacy learning topics, activities, procedures, and products.
9. Use collaborative learning groups where positive relationships among children are planned and monitored.
10. Monitor and control the amount of perceived failure children experience.
11. Break tasks into parts according to difficulty, where success on earlier portions can balance failures on more difficult portions.
12. Allow children to correct and improve work, turning possible failures into successes thorough effort.
13. Help children learn to invoke more effort and practice when they perceive that they have failed.
14. Teach children the thinking-related and emotional/valuing vocabulary related to motivation.
15. Group together children of similar languages and similar ethnic groups for some activities.

References

Atkinson, J. W. (1964). *An introduction to motivation.* Princeton, NJ: Van Nostrand.

Auerbach, S. (2010). Beyond coffee with the principal: Toward leadership for authentic school-family partnerships. *Journal of School Leadership, 20*, 728–757.

August, D., & Hakuta, K. (Eds.). (1997). *Improving schooling for language-minority children: A research agenda.* Washington, DC: National Academy Press.

August, D., & Shanahan, T. (Eds.). (2008). *Developing reading and writing in second-language learners* (pp. 131–250). New York, NY: Routledge.

Aukrust, V. G., & Rydland, V. (2011). Preschool classroom conversations as long-term resources for second language and literacy acquisition. *Journal of Applied Developmental Psychology, 32*, 198–207.

Barnett, W. S., Yarosz, D. J., Thomas, J., Jung, K., & Blanco, D. (2007). Two-way and monolingual English immersion in preschool education: An experimental comparison. *Early Childhood Research Quarterly, 22*, 277–293.

Benner, A. D., & Crosnoe, R. (2011). The racial/ethnic composition of elementary schools and young children's academic and socioemotional functioning. *American Educational Research Journal, 48*, 621–646.

Bianco, M., Bressoux, P., Doyen, A. L., Lambert, E., Lima, L., Pellenq, C., & Zorman, M. (2010). Early training in oral comprehension and phonological skills: Results of a three-year longitudinal study. *Scientific Studies of Reading, 14*, 211–246.

Biemiller, A., & Boote, C. (2006). An effective method for building meaning vocabulary in primary grades. *Journal of Educational Psychology, 98*, 44–62.

Boyer, N., & Ehri, L. C. (2011). Contribution of phonemic segmentation instruction with letters and articulation pictures to word reading and spelling in beginners. *Scientific Studies of Reading, 15*, 440–470.

Bradley, R. H., & Cervyn, R. F. (2002). Socioeconomic status and child development. *Annual Review of Psychology, 53*, 371–399.

Branum-Martin, L., Foorman, B. R., Francis, D. J., & Mehta, P. D. (2010). Contextual effects of bilingual programs on beginning reading. *Journal of Educational Psychology, 102*, 341–355.

Brown, C. (1998). The role of the L1 grammar in the L2 acquisition of segmental structure. *Second Language Research, 14*, 136–193.

Brown, M. (1942). *The runaway bunny.* New York, NY: Harper and Row.

Burchinal, M. et al. (2012). Instruction in Spanish in prekindergarten and child outcomes for English language learners. *Early Childhood Research Quarterly, 27*, 188–197.

Caplan, N., Chou, M. H., & Whitmore, J. K. (1991). *Children of the boat people: A study of educational success.* Ann Arbor, MI: University of Michigan Press.

Chang, F., Crawford, G., Early, D., Bryant, D., Howes, C., Burchinal, M., . . . & Pianta, R. (2007). Spanish-speaking children's social and language development in prekindergarten classrooms. *Early Education and Development, 18,* 243–269.

Chang, F., & Burns, B. M. (2005). Attention in preschoolers: Association with effortful control and motivation. *Child Development, 76,* 247-263.

Chapman, J. W., & Tunmer, W. E. (1997). Development of young children's reading self-concepts: An examination of emerging subcomponents and their relationship with reading achievement. *Journal of Educational Psychology, 87,* 154–167.

Chapman, J. W., Tunmer, W. E., & Prochnow, J. E. (2000). Early reading-related skills and performance, reading self-concept, and the development of academic self-concept: A longitudinal study. *Journal of Educational Psychology, 92,* 703–708.

Chesterfield, R. A., Chesterfield, K. B., Hayes-Latimer, K., & Chavez, R. (1983). The influence of peers and teachers on second language acquisition in preschool programs. *TESOL Quarterly, 17,* 401–419.

Cirino, P., Pollard-Durodola, S., Foorman, B., Carlson, C., & Francis, D. (2007). Teacher characteristics, classroom instruction, and student literacy and language outcomes in bilingual kindergartners. *The Elementary School Journal, 107,* 341–364.

Claessens, A., Engel, M., & Curran, F. C. (2014). Academic content, student learning, and the persistence of preschool effects. *American Educational Research Journal, 51,* 403–434.

Crosnoe, R. (2004). Double disadvantage or signs of resilience? The elementary school contexts of children from Mexican immigrant families. *American Educational Research Journal, 42,* 269–303.

Cummins, J. (2000). *Language, power, and pedagogy: Bilingual children in the crossfire.* Clevedon, England: Multilingual Matters.

Cunningham, A. E., Etter, K., Platas, L., Wheeler, S., & Campbell, K. (2015). Professional development in emergent literacy: A design experiment of teacher study groups. *Early Childhood Research Quarterly, 31,* 62–77.

Cunningham, A. E., & Stanovich, K. E. (1997). Early reading acquisition and its relation to reading experience and ability 10 years later. *Developmental Psychology, 33*(6), 934.

deBrunhoff, J. (1932). *The travels of Babar.* New York, NY: Random House.

Dickinson, D. K. (2011). Teachers' language practices and academic outcomes of preschool children. *Science, 333,* 964–967.

Dweck, C. S. (1975). The role of expectations and attributions in the alleviation of learned helplessness. *Journal of Personality and Social Psychology, 31*(4), 674–685.

Dweck, C. S. (1986). Motivational processes affecting learning. *American Psychologist, 41,*1040–1048.

Dweck, C. S. (2002). The development of ability conceptions. In A. Wigfield & J. Eccles (Eds.), *Development of achievement motivation* (pp. 57–88). San Diego, CA: Academic Press.

Eccles, J., & Wigfield, A. (2002). Motivational beliefs, values, and goals. *Annual Review of Psychology, 53,* 109–132.

Eccles, J., Wigfield, A., Harold, R., & Blumenfeld, P. B. (1993). Age and gender differences in children's self- and task-perceptions during elementary school. *Child Development, 64,* 830–847.

Editorial Progress in Education Research Center. (2009). Analysis of the U.S. Census Bureau's American Community Survey (2005–2007). Retrieved from http://www.edweek.org

Elbro, C. (1996). Early linguistic abilities and reading development: A review and a hypothesis. *Reading and Writing: An Interdisciplinary Journal, 8*, 453–485.

Ellis, R. (2005). Principles of instructed language learning. *System, 33,* 209–224.

Espinosa, L. M. (2006). Social, cultural, and linguistic features of school readiness in young Latino children. In B. Bowman & E. K. Moore (Eds.), *School readiness and social-emotional Development* (pp. 33–47). Washington, DC: National Black Child Development Institute, Inc.

Gamez, P. B. (2015). Classroom-based English exposure and English language learners' expressive language skills. *Early Childhood Research Quarterly, 31,* 135–146.

Genesee, F., Lindholm-Leary, K., Saunders, W., & Christian, D. (2006). *Educating English language learners: A synthesis of research evidence.* Cambridge, England: Cambridge University Press.

Geva E., Yaghoub-Zadeh, Z., & Schuster, B. (2000). Understanding individual difference in word recognition skills in ESL children. *Annals of dyslexia, 50*, 121–154.

Goldenberg, C. (2008). Teaching English language learners: What the research does—and does not—say. *American Educator, 32* (8–23), 42–44.

Greene, J. (1997). A meta-analysis of the Rossell and Baker review of bilingual education research. *Bilingual Research Journal, 21,* 103–122.

Guthrie, J. T., & Wigfield, A. (2000). Engagement and motivation in reading. In M. Kamil, P. D. Pearson, & R. Barr (Eds.), *Handbook of reading research* (Vol. III, pp. 503–524). Mahwah, NJ: Erlbaum.

Hakuta, K., Butler, Y. G., & Witt, D. (2000). How long does it take English learners to attain proficiency? The University of California Linguistic Minority Research Institute. Policy report 2000-1. *Adolescence, 40*, 503-512.

Harter, S. (1974). Pleasure derived by children from cognitive challenge and mastery. *Child Development, 45,* 661–669.

Harter, S. (1978). Effectance motivation reconsidered: Toward a developmental model. *Human Development, 21,* 34–64.

Head Start. (n.d.). Snapshot of references to dual language learners (DLLs) in state early learning guidelines. Retrieved from eclkc.ohs.acf.hhs.gov/hslc/tta-system/cultural-linguistic/state-guidelines/snapshot.html

Heitin, L. (2016). The search for Common-Core curricula: Where are teachers finding materials? *Education Week*. Retrieved from http://blogs.edweek.org/edweek/curriculum/2016/04/common_core_curricula_teacher_materials.html?cmp=eml-enl-cco-news1-RM

Hiebert, E. H., & Mesmer, H. A. (2013). Upping the ante of text complexity in the Common Core State Standards examining its potential impact on young readers. *Educational Researcher, 42,* 44–51.

Hindman, A. H., & Wasik, B. A. (2015). Building vocabulary in two languages: An examination of Spanish-speaking Dual Language Learners in Head Start. *Early Childhood Research Quarterly, 31,* 19–33.

Hoover, W. A., & Gough, P. B. (1990). The simple view of reading. *Reading and writing, 2,* 127–160.

Joshi, M., Binks, E., Graham, L., Ocker-Dean, E., Smith, D., & Boulware-Gooden, R. (2009). Do textbooks used in university reading education courses conform to the instructional recommendations of the National Reading Panel? *Journal of Learning Disabilities, 42,* 458–463.

Karabenick, S. A., & Noda, P. A. (2004). Professional development implications of teachers' beliefs and attitudes toward English language learners. *Bilingual Research Journal, 28,* 55–75.

Kieffer, M. J. (2012). Early oral language and later reading development in Spanish-speaking English language learners: Evidence from a nine-year longitudinal study. *Journal of Applied Developmental Psychology, 33,* 146–157.

Kim, Y. K., Hutchison, L. A., & Winsler, A. (2013). Bilingual education in the United States: An historical overview and examination of two-way immersion. *Educational Review, 67,* 236–252.

Lepola, J., Poskiparta, E., Laakkonen, E., & Niemi, P. (2005). Development of and relationship between phonological and motivational processes and naming speed in predicting word recognition in grade 1. *Scientific Studies of Reading, 9,* 367–399.

Lesaux, N., & Siegel, L. (2003). The development of reading in children who speak English as a second language. *Developmental Psychology, 39,* 1005–1009.

López, M. G., & Tashakkori, A. (2006). Differential outcomes of two bilingual education programs on English language learners. *Bilingual Research Journal, 30,* 123–145.

Lucas T. (2011). Language, schooling, and the preparation of teachers for linguistic diversity. In T. Lucas (Ed.), *Teacher preparation for linguistically diverse classrooms: A resource for teacher educators* (pp. 3–17). New York, NY: Routledge.

Mages, W. K. (2008). Does creative drama promote language development in early childhood? A review of the methods and measures employed in the empirical literature. *Review of Educational Research, 78,* 124–152.

Markus, H. R., & Kitayama, S. (1991). Culture and the self: Implications for cognition, emotion, and motivation. *Psychological Review, 98,* 224.

Marulis, L. M., & Neuman, S. B. (2013). How vocabulary interventions affect young children at risk: A meta-analytic review. *Journal of Research on Educational Effectiveness, 6,* 223–262.

Mashburn, A. J., Pianta, R. C., Hamre, B. K., Downer, J. T., Barbarin, O. A., Bryant, D., et al. (2008). Measures of classroom quality in prekindergarten and children's development of academic, language and social skills. *Child Development, 79,* 732–749.

Master, A., & Walton, G. M. (2013). Minimal groups increase young children's motivation and learning on group-relevant tasks. *Child Development, 84,* 737–751.

McLoyd, V. C. (1998). Socioeconomic disadvantage and child development. *American Psychologist, 53,* 185–204.

Moats, L. (2015). Still wanted: Teachers with knowledge of language. *Journal of Learning Disabilities, 42,* 387–391.

Moll, L. C., Amanti, C., Neff, D., & Gonzalez, N. (1992). Funds of knowledge for teaching: Using a qualitative approach to connect homes and classrooms. *Theory into Practice, 31,* 132–141

Nagy, W. E., Herman, P. A., & Anderson, R. C. (1985). Learning words from context. *Reading Research Quarterly,* 233-253.

Nassaji, H. (2014). The role and importance of lower-level processes in second language reading. *Language Teaching, 47,* 1–37.

Nassaji, H., & Fotos, S. (2011). *Teaching grammar in second language classrooms.* New York, NY: Routledge.

National Association for the Education of Young Children. (1995). Responding to linguistic and cultural diversity: Recommendations for effective early childhood education. A position statement of the National Association for the Education of Young Children. Washington, DC: Author.

National Center for Education Statistics. (2015). *The nation's report card: A first look: 2013 mathematics and reading* (NCES 2014-451). Washington, DC: Institute of Education Sciences, U.S. Department of Education.

National Clearinghouse for English Language Acquisition. (2012). *The growing numbers of limited English proficient students.* Washington, DC: Author. Retrieved from http://www.ncela.us/files/fast_facts/OELA_FF_NAEP_LineTrends.pdf

National Governors Association Center for Best Practices, & Council of Chief State School Officers. (2010). Common Core State Standards for English language arts and literacy in history/social studies, science, and technical subjects. Washington, DC: Authors. Retrieved from www.corestandards.org/assets/CCSSI_ELA%20Standards.pdf

Report of the national reading panel: Teaching children to read: An evidence-based assessment of the scientific research literature on reading and its implications for reading instruction: Reports of the subgroups. (2000). Washington, DC: National Institute of Child Health and Human Development, National Institutes of Health.

NICHD Early Child Care Research Network. (2005). Pathways to reading: The role of oral language in the transition to reading. *Developmental Psychology, 41*, 428–442.

Ngo, B., & Lee, S. J. (2007). Complicating the image of model minority success: A review of Southeast Asian American education. Review of Educational Research, 77, 415–453.

Ogden, C. K. (1930). *Basic English: A general introduction with rules and grammar.* London, England: Kegan Paul, Trench, Trubner and Co. Ltd.

Palermo, F., Mikulski, A. M., Fabes, R. A., Hanish, L. D., Martin, C. L., & Stargel, L. E. (2014). English exposure in the home and classroom: Predictions to Spanish-speaking preschoolers' English vocabulary skills. *Applied Psycholinguistics, 35,* 1163–1187.

Phillips, B. M., Menchetti, J. C., & Lonigan, C. J. (2008). Successful phonological awareness instruction with preschool children: Lessons from the classroom. *Topics in Early Childhood Special Education, 28*, 3–17.

Poarch, G. J., & Bialystok, E. (2015). Bilingualism as a model for multitasking. *Developmental Review, 35*, 113–124.

Porter, A., McMaken, J., Hwang, J., & Yang, R. (2011). Common Core Standards: The new U.S. intended curriculum. *Educational Researcher, 40,* 103–116.

Portes, A., & Hao, L. (2002). The price of uniformity: Language, family, and personality adjustment in the immigrant second generation. *Ethnic and Racial Studies, 25,* 889–912.

Pufahl, I., & Rhodes, N. C. (2011). Foreign language instruction in U.S. schools: Results of a national survey of elementary and secondary schools. *Foreign Language Annals, 44,* 258–288.

Raluca, B. R., Bialystok, E., Castro, D. C., & Sanchez, E., M. (2014). The cognitive development of young dual language learners: A critical review. *Early Childhood Research Quarterly, 29*, 699–714.

Ready, D. D., & Wright, D. L. (2011). Accuracy and inaccuracy in teachers' perceptions of young children's cognitive abilities: The role of child background and classroom context. *American Educational Research Journal, 48*, 335–360.

Reeve, J. R., Deci, E. L., & Ryan, R. M. (2004). Self-determination theory: A dialectical framework for understanding sociocultural influences on student motivation, In D. M. McEnery & S. V. Eaten (Eds.), *Big theories revisited* (pp. 31-60). Greenwich, CT: Information Age.

Rjosk, C., Richter, D., Hochweber, J., Lüdtke, O., & Stanat, P. (2015). Classroom composition and language minority students' motivation in language lessons. *Journal of Educational Psychology, 107*, 1171–1185.

Roberts, T. A. (2005). Articulation accuracy and vocabulary size contributions to phonemic awareness and word reading in English language learners. *Journal of Educational Psychology, 97*, 601–616.

Roberts, T. A. (2008). Home storybook reading in primary or second language with preschool children: Evidence of equal effectiveness for second-language vocabulary acquisition. *Reading Research Quarterly, 43*, 103–130.

Roberts, T. A. (2011). Preschool foundations for reading and writing success. In R. O'Connor & P. Vadasy (Eds.), *Handbook of reading interventions* (pp. 27–62). New York, NY: Guilford Press.

Roberts, T. A. (2013). Opportunities and oversights within the Common Core State Standards for English learners' language and literacy achievement. In S. B. Neuman & L. B. Gambrell (Eds.), *Quality reading instruction in the age of common core standards* (pp. 90–106). Newark, DE: International Reading Association.

Roberts, T. A. (2014). Not so silent after all: Examination and analysis of the silent stage in childhood second language acquisition. *Early Childhood Research Quarterly, 29*, 22–40.

Roberts, T. A., Christo, C., & Shefelbine, J. A. (2010). Word recognition. In M. Kamil, P. D. Pearson, E. Moje, & P. Afflerbach (Eds.), *Handbook of reading research* (Vol. IV, pp. 229–258). New York, NY: Routledge.

Rolstad, K., Mahoney, K., & Glass, G. (2005). The big picture: A meta-analysis of program effectiveness research on English language learners. *Educational Policy, 19*, 572–594.

Rosenthal, J., & Ehri, L. C. (2008). The mnemonic value of orthography for vocabulary learning. *Journal of Educational Psychology, 100*, 175–191.

Saunders, W. M., Foorman, B. R., & Carlson, C. D. (2006). Is a separate block of time for oral? English language development in programs for English learners needed? *The Elementary School Journal, 107*, 181–198.

Schiefele, U. (2001). Interest and learning from text. *Scientific Studies of Reading, 3*, 257–279.

Shanahan, T., Callison, K., Carriere, C., Duke, N. K., Pearson, P. D., Schatschneider, C., & Torgesen, J. (2010). *Improving reading comprehension in kindergarten through 3rd grade: A practice guide* (NCEE 2010-4038). Washington, DC: National Center for Education Evaluation and Regional Assistance, Institute of Education Sciences, U.S. Department of Education. Retrieved from whatworks.ed.gov/publications/practice guides

Sinclair, J. (Ed.). (2002). *Collins COBUILD Student's Dictionary*. Glasgow, Scotland: HarperCollins.

Slavin, R., & Cheung, A. (2005). A synthesis of research on language of reading instruction for English language learners. *Review of Educational Research, 75*, 247–281.

Solari, E. J., & Gerber, M. M. (2008). Early comprehension instruction for Spanish speaking ELLs: Teaching text level reading skills while maintaining effects on word level skills. *Learning Disabilities Research & Practice, 23*, 155–168.

Stipek, D. J., Roberts, T. A., & Sanborn, M. E. (1984). Pre-school age children's performance expectations for themselves and another child as a function of the incentive value of success and the salience of past performance. *Child Development, 55*, 1983–1989.

Swain, M. (2005). The output hypothesis: Theory and research. In E. Hinkel (Ed.), *Handbook of research in second language teaching and learning* (Vol. 1, pp. 471–483). Mahwah, NJ: Erlbaum.

US Department of Health and Human Services. (2010). Revisiting and Updating the Multicultural Principles for Head Start Programs Serving Children Ages Birth to Five. Washington, DC: Office of Head Start.

U.S. Department of Health and Human Services, Administration for Children and Families. (2012). *The benefits of being bilingual.* Washington, DC: Office of Head Start. Retrieved from from http://eclkc.ohs.acf.hhs.gov/hslc/tta-system/cultural-linguistic/docs/benefits-of-being-bilingual.pdf

Vadasy, P. F., & Sanders, E. A. (2015). Incremental learning of difficult words in story contexts: The role of spelling and pronouncing new vocabulary. *Reading and Writing: An Interdisciplinary Journal, 28,* 371–394.

van den Broek, P., & Espin, C. A. (2012. Connecting cognitive theory and assessment: Measuring individual differences in reading comprehension. *School Psychology Review, 41,* 315–325.

White, R. W. (1959). Motivation reconsidered: the concept of competence. *Psychological Review, 66,* 297–333.

Wigfield, A., Eccles, J. S., Roesser, R., & Schiefele, U. (2008). Development of achievement motivation. In W. Damon & R. Lerner (Eds.), *Child and adolescent development: An advanced course.* New York, NY: Wiley & Sons.

Williams, J., Kao, J., Pao, L., Ordynans, J., Atkins, J., et al. (2016). Close analysis of texts with structure (cats): An intervention to teach reading comprehension to at-risk second graders. *Journal of Educational Psychology, 108,* 1061–1077.

Willig, A. (1985). A meta-analysis of selected studies on the effectiveness of bilingual education. *Review of Educational Research, 55,* 269–317.

Winsler, A., Kim, Y. K., & Richard, E. R. (2014). Socio-emotional skills, behavior problems, and Spanish competence predict the acquisition of English among English learners in poverty. *Developmental Psychology, 50,* 2242–22

Wright, T. S. (2012). What classroom observations reveal about oral vocabulary instruction in kindergarten. *Reading Research Quarterly, 47,* 353–355.

Wright, T. S., & Neuman, S. B. (2013). Vocabulary instruction in commonly used kindergarten core curricula. *The Elementary School Journal, 113,* 386–408.

Index

About the Author

Theresa A. Roberts is currently a senior research associate at the Oregon Research Institute and an independent consultant for PreK–Grade 2 professional and programmatic development in literacy for English-fluent and emergent bilingual children. She conducts classroom-based research on vocabulary learning and reading foundations. Her most recent research, funded by a grant from the United States Institute of Education Science (IES), is designed to determine the most effective classroom instruction for teaching preschool children the alphabet. She is a professor emeritus at the California State University, Sacramento.

The Common Core State Standards in Literacy Series

A series designed to help educators successfully implement CCSS literacy standards in K–12 classrooms

Susan B. Neuman and D. Ray Reutzel, Editors

Series board: Diane August, Linda Gambrell, Steve Graham, Laura Justice, Margaret McKeown, and Timothy Shanahan

---

Literacy Success for Emergent Bilinguals
Getting It Right in the PreK–2 Classroom
Theresa A. Roberts

Teaching Skills for Complex Text
Deepening Close Reading in the Classroom
Heidi Anne E. Mesmer

Professional Learning in Action
An Inquiry Approach for Teachers of Literacy
Victoria J. Risko & MaryEllen Vogt

Young Meaning Makers—Teaching Comprehension, Grades K–2
D. Ray Reutzel, Sarah K. Clark, Cindy D. Jones, & Sandra L. Gillam

Revitalizing Read Alouds
Interactive Talk About Books with Young Children, PreK–2
Lisa Hammett Price & Barbara A. Bradley

RTI in the Common Core Classroom
A Framework for Instruction and Assessment
Sharon Vaughn, Philip Capin, Garrett J. Roberts, & Melodee A. Walker

The Fluency Factor
Authentic Instruction and Assessment for Reading Success in the Common Core Classroom
Timothy Rasinski & James K. Nageldinger

Helping English Learners to Write—Meeting Common Core Standards, Grades 6–12
Carol Booth Olson, Robin C. Scarcella, & Tina Matuchniak

Reading Across Multiple Texts in the Common Core Classroom, K–5
Janice A. Dole, Brady E. Donaldson, & Rebecca S. Donaldson

Reading, Thinking, and Writing About History
Teaching Argument Writing to Diverse Learners in the Common Core Classroom, Grades 6–12
Chauncey Monte-Sano, Susan De La Paz, & Mark Felton

Engaging Students in Disciplinary Literacy, K–6
Reading, Writing, and Teaching Tools for the Classroom
Cynthia H. Brock, Virginia J. Goatley, Taffy E. Raphael, Elisabeth Trost-Shahata, & Catherine M. Weber

All About Words
Increasing Vocabulary in the Common Core Classroom, PreK–2
Susan B. Neuman & Tanya Wright